tray to make a lovely centerpiece." *Mark Wink* ... *n Director* ✕ "I fill salt and pepper shakers from my collection with a variety of spices that complement the dishes being served—such as spicy seasoning for a chili party, cinnamon to top off a slice of apple pie, or cocoa powder on top of a creamy dessert. That way, people can sprinkle on as much extra flavor as they want." *Natalie Ermann, Assistant Managing Editor* ✕ "Any dessert put on a cake stand always looks more yummy!" *Rebecca Robertson, Assistant Collecting Editor* ✕ "I have been collecting napkin rings for many years—mostly antique, mostly silver, all different. I love the way they look on the table when I entertain. It's also fun to figure out which napkin ring is most appropriate for each guest, based on his or her personality and style." *Helen Seligman, Associate Publisher* ✕ "I compile my own mixed CDs so that I don't have to worry about the music ending or getting monotonous at a party. I have something for cocktail hour, another to play during the meal, something for coffee and dessert, and one that will let guests know when it's time to leave!" *Christopher Raymond, Business Systems Analyst* ✕

GOOD THINGS
for EASY ENTERTAINING

GOOD THINGS
for EASY ENTERTAINING

FROM THE EDITORS *of* MARTHA STEWART LIVING

Contents

INTRODUCTION With the hectic schedules that dictate so many of our days, it's a wonder anyone still entertains. But gathering with family and friends can provide a much-needed respite from busy lives and overbooked calendars. It doesn't matter what sort of party you host—a buffet or seated dinner, brunch or cocktails, in the kitchen or on the porch—it's spending time together that's important. With a bit of planning, you will not only have the time to put together a successful party, but also join in the fun yourself.

This book gathers many of our favorite "Good Things," clever yet achievable ideas and projects. We organized the Good Things in the order in which your guests will most likely encounter them. Drinks and hors d'oeuvres, with recipes and suggestions for presentation, come first. Several chapters on other elements of entertaining follow, including how to provide practical and decorative lighting, arrange centerpieces, dress the table, and create welcoming place cards. You will also find simple and satisfying desserts to top off any meal. Finally, we offer useful tips and techniques to help guide you through a party from start to finish, including how to organize ingredients while cooking and the best method for removing candle wax from a tabletop. Throughout the book, look for expert advice from Susan Spungen (pictured at the head of the table, opposite page, bottom center), editorial director of MARTHA STEWART LIVING's food department.

If you like, follow our instructions to the letter. Adorn a white tablecloth with colorful leaf prints, for example, or make a set of waterproof coasters with a piece of oilcloth. Or remake them with your own sense of style: Instead of the flowers shown, substitute some that you cut from your garden; bring an outdoor lighting idea inside. Above all, just remember the key to easy entertaining: Keep it simple and enjoyable for everyone.

No. 1

DRINKS

Whatever the style of your event, you'll want to offer something to drink as soon as guests arrive. You might serve a specialty cocktail or provide a choice of several. Many people prefer nonalcoholic refreshments, so be prepared to make a few. Of course, you should also plan which beverages will accompany the meal and whether you'll be serving anything after dinner. Following are suggestions for both warm and cold drinks, with liquor and without, blended and on the rocks. You'll also find interesting but simple presentations: Papaya spears garnish smoothies; chilled sake is served in cucumber cups; tiny handwritten name tags attached to wineglass stems help everyone identify his or her drink—and cut down on the number of glasses to wash when the party is over.

OPPOSITE: *Homemade parasols, set in tumblers of icy lemonade, are created with assorted origami paper and wooden skewers. These cheerful, easy-to-make tops can gently shade all your summer drinks. For umbrella how-to, see page 16.*

FROZEN BLOODY MARYS

Although many believe the Bloody Mary was named for the British Queen of the same epithet, it may well have been invented in a Paris bar in the 1920s in honor of a woman from Chicago. The varieties shown above take their distinctive colors from yellow, orange, and red tomatoes, and their slushy consistency from a whirl in the blender. Small tomatoes, basil leaves, and cubed mozzarella make tasty garnishes. SEE THE RECIPES

CUCUMBER SAKE CUPS

Cucumbers are transformed into boxy little cups for shots of chilled sake, the Japanese rice wine. To make cups, slice ends off an English cucumber, which has few seeds and little pulp, then slice crosswise into three 2-inch sections. Stand one at a time on its base; square sides of cucumber, reserving skin. With an apple corer, hollow out center, leaving about $1/2$ inch at bottom. Cut reserved skin into matchsticks for garnish.

ROSY CHAMPAGNE PUNCH

Celebrate any occasion with this festive and eye-catching drink. Fill a small ice bucket halfway with ice. To make four 4 1/2-ounce servings, pour 3 tablespoons of grenadine, 3 tablespoons of Cointreau, 2 tablespoons of brandy, and 1 3/4 cups of Champagne over the ice. Stir gently, and ladle the punch into four wide-mouthed stemmed glasses. If desired, garnish with raspberries, apple slices, or other seasonal fruit.

LEMON MINT JULEPS ON ICE

First made famous when served in silver cups at the running of the Kentucky Derby, mint juleps consist of bourbon, simple syrup, fresh mint, and crushed ice. Our lemony variation is great for a casual buffet on a lazy afternoon. The glasses are filled to the rim and topped with mint sprigs, then set in a bed of crushed ice in a footed glass bowl so guests can help themselves throughout the party. SEE THE RECIPES

SERVING DRINKS

People often worry that they have to offer a full bar when having a party, but it is perfectly acceptable to limit the number of options.

The variety of drinks you offer depends on the kind of party you're having. While a sit-down dinner party might require more choices, at a shorter, casual get-together I usually serve beer, wine, and possibly one hard liquor (vodka mixes well with lots of things) or a specialty drink. Place a bottle of vodka next to pitchers of cranberry juice, soda, tonic, and if it's a summer party, lemonade; this also provides alternatives for guests who don't wish to drink alcohol.

Specialty drinks such as margaritas or Pimm's cups—whether mixed in a blender or stirred in a pitcher—are always popular. They add to the festive atmosphere of a party and can contribute to an overall theme.

To avoid congestion, place the "bar" (which may be improvised on a counter or tabletop) in an area that has room for circulation. If it is self-service, make sure that everything guests need to help themselves—bottle openers, ice tongs, garnishes—is on hand. Place glasses and containers of ice on trays to catch drips and spills, and open and re-cork enough wine so that guests won't have to open bottles themselves. Prepare garnishes in advance, and make sure you have enough of them—many garnishes are more than decorative, adding a flavor component to the drink. —SUSAN SPUNGEN

MADE-TO-ORDER LEMONADE

Some like their lemonade sweet and others prefer it tart, so let everyone mix a glass to his own taste. Provide separate containers of fresh lemon juice, simple syrup, and water, along with glasses, ice, and stirrers. A good starting point is one part juice to two parts syrup and three parts water. Prepare the simple syrup ahead by bringing equal parts sugar and water to a boil until sugar has completely dissolved; let cool.

FRUIT SHAKES These refreshing smoothies have an exotic twist: They are inspired by those served at Vietnamese restaurants. Delightful with a light meal or as a snack or dessert, they are made from condensed milk, crushed ice, sugar, and the fruit or vegetable of your choice (we used, from left to right, avocado, mango, and papaya). Pour into tall glasses, such as the fountain glasses shown here; garnish with a mint sprig or slice of fruit, and serve with a straw. SEE THE RECIPES

COLORFUL COASTERS Painted oilcloth was once a household staple. Today's printed versions are versatile and easy to work with—their cut edges won't fray—and their patterned designs suggest cheerful cutouts for waterproof coasters. To make large floral shapes, simply cut along the outline of a single bloom; cut other shapes using scallop-edge shears. Back each coaster with a solid-colored piece of oilcloth cut to the same shape and size. Coat the reverse side of each piece lightly with spray adhesive, and press together with your hands. Trim final shape and, if desired, machine-stitch edges, leaving a small seam allowance. These coasters bloom under some of our favorite chilled drinks: Meyer Lemon Drops (left front and rear), a Peachmopolitan (right front), and a frozen Pink Salty Dog (far right). SEE THE RECIPES

PLANTER ICE BUCKETS On a hot day, just before guests arrive, stand bottles of well-chilled beer and wine in galvanized planters at the center of the dining table. For a long table, set one planter at either end, separated by a flower arrangement. Fill planters with shaved ice. To prevent leaks, seal inside seams of planters with clear silicone sealant, following manufacturer's instructions. The metal will still sweat, but with such ready access to cold drinks, your guests will not.

DRINK UMBRELLAS HOW-TO

MATERIALS: *soup can, assorted origami paper, pinking shears or scallop-edge shears, glue stick or double-sided tape, craft glue, wooden skewers.* Use a soup can as a template to trace circles onto the back of origami paper. Cut paper with pinking shears or scallop-edge shears for a decorative edge. From each circle, remove a wedge measuring about $\frac{1}{8}$ of circumference. Fashion into a cone, lightly overlapping straight ends; use a glue stick or tape to secure. Dab craft glue inside point of cone, and pierce tip with a wooden skewer (snip base of skewer if necessary).

DRINK TAGS

To help guests keep track of their wineglasses or other stemware, make name tags out of construction paper with leaf-shaped punches (available at crafts stores), or cut your own shapes with scissors. Write names on the tags, and use a $\frac{1}{8}$-inch hole punch to make small holes near one end. Thread waxed twine through holes; loop twine around glass stems and knot.

POM-POM SKEWERS

MATERIALS: *metallic wrapping paper, scissors, wooden skewers, double-sided tape.*
Create fireworks at your next party with swizzle sticks rolled in metallic paper fringe. Cut strips of lightweight metallic wrapping paper, each 2 inches wide and 12 inches long. Make deep, narrowly spaced cuts along one long side of strip, leaving a $1/2$-inch border (below). Starting at one end, wrap border of strip around top of wooden skewer; secure with double-sided tape. Trim skewers to fit neatly in glass, with 1 to 2 inches extending above the rim. Shake to fluff fringe.

Warm drinks are as versatile as they are rejuvenating: They can be perfect as an accompaniment to a midday meal or on their own as a nightcap. Serve them in well-insulated glasses, or those with handles, so they're not too hot to hold.

WARM SPICED LEMONADE

BELOW: Keep this hot beverage in mind when you want to offer a quick warm-up. In a 4-quart saucepan, combine 9 cups water, 1 cup fresh lemon juice, 2 cups orange juice, 2 cups sugar, 1 tablespoon pure vanilla extract, and $1/8$ tablespoon ground cloves; simmer to let flavors meld. Serve lemonade hot; or make ahead, refrigerate, and reheat. This recipe makes about 3 quarts.

CRANBERRY CIDER

ABOVE: Cranberries give this "cider" its rosy color, which is especially suited to Christmas and Valentine's Day. Made from cranberry juice mulled with sticks of cinnamon, fresh ginger, and the juice of an orange, the cider is strained and served hot, straight from the stove.

SEE THE RECIPES

COFFEE WITH COGNAC AND CARDAMOM

Similar to Irish coffee in its frothiness, this hot elixir makes a bracing after-dinner drink for a cold evening. Brandy and strong coffee are combined with a sweet cardamom syrup that can be made up to a week ahead. Fill tall, clear glasses halfway with the coffee, and top with freshly whipped cream.

SEE THE RECIPES

No. 2

HORS D'OEUVRES

Imagine the perfect party food; chances are, your mind conjures up all sorts of savory bite-size delights. Hors d'oeuvres are, after all, the first foray into any well-planned menu. They ought to pack enough pleasure into each mouthful to tempt guests' taste buds and tide them over until dinner. Or, if you're throwing a cocktail party, the offerings should include a satisfying assortment of flavors, textures, and styles. What follows is a collection of quick hors d'oeuvre classics—nothing that will trip you up or send you rushing to the market at the last minute. Instead, you'll come to rely on these favorite crowd pleasers again and again. Pass them on trays or leave them in a spot where guests can help themselves. Just make sure not to put out too many, lest you spoil anyone's appetite.

OPPOSITE: *Guests can take their pick of miniature quiches—bacon and onion, or tomato and niçoise olive. They are baked in 4-inch bottomless ring molds and then quartered before serving to make them bite-size. See The Recipes.*

SAVORY TARTLETS

BELOW: Surround a selection of small olive tartlets with an olive-leaf wreath for an especially pleasing presentation. Dollops of goat cheese and halved olives are placed on top of puff-pastry rounds before the tartlets are baked. The wreath is formed from the tips of olive branches, loosely braided to follow the curve of the platter and then finished with a satin bow.

SEE THE RECIPES

WARM OLIVES

RIGHT: Offering a selection of warm herbed olives is a lovely start to any party. One-half pound of olives serves about 6 people. Rinse the olives, drain, and place in an oven-proof baking dish. Toss with olive oil and flavorings of your choice. We paired olives with (from top) hot chili peppers and garlic cloves; bay leaves and fennel seeds; and lemon peel and thyme leaves. Cook 15 to 25 minutes at 350°F.

ANTIPASTO

OPPOSITE: A platter filled with sausages, cheeses, breads, and vegetables is ideal for cocktail hour and involves little more on the host's part than opening packages and jars. Tightly wrapped in plastic, cheeses and cured meats will last several weeks in the refrigerator. Unopened jars of olives, caperberries, and anchovies will keep for months. If you insist on going to a bit more trouble, you can roast a few peppers and marinate some artichoke hearts yourself.

GOUGERES

Gougères are baked pâte-à-choux puffs flavored with cheese (most often Gruyère, but we used Manchego). Pâte à choux is quite different from other pastry—it is prepared on top of the stove first, then the dough is usually piped from a pastry bag before being baked. As a bonus to the busy host, gougères can be formed ahead of time, then frozen in a single layer in a plastic bag and baked just before serving. SEE THE RECIPES

CHEESE COINS

Cheddar lovers will fall for the flavor of these cheese coins. The baked crackers are topped with jalapeño jelly, a wonderful complement to their sharp flavor and crumbly texture. They are just the right size for guests to pop into their mouths without fussing over second bites or toppling ingredients. The dough is formed into easy-to-slice logs and keeps in the freezer for up to one month. SEE THE RECIPES

GARDEN-HARVEST TEMPURA

Turn vegetables from the garden (or supermarket) into tempura, light and crispy Japanese fritters. Mix the simple batter and then chill it—ice-cold batter is the secret to successful frying. Slice vegetables, such as carrots, leeks, squash, and red bell peppers, into thin pieces for quick and even cooking (keep green beans, baby beets, and baby eggplants whole). Coat with the batter, fry, and serve with dipping sauce. SEE THE RECIPES

EDAMAME

This traditional Japanese snack is among the simplest to prepare. Edamame (Japanese for soybeans) are available in the freezer section of most supermarkets and in Asian markets from late spring to early fall. Boil briefly until crisp-tender, drain, and dust with coarse salt. Serve additional salt on the side. Since the beans are stripped from the pods, set out a separate bowl (or leave room on a platter) for discarded pods.

SPICED NUTS

BELOW: Pecans, walnuts, almonds, and cashews make addictive cocktail snacks when tossed with spices and baked until crunchy and golden. Set them out in the middle of a coffee table or along the bar area, within easy reach of guests. You can vary the type of nuts you serve, making a mixed batch or several dishes of individual varieties. SEE THE RECIPES

ROASTED RED PEPPER DIP

ABOVE: This simple sauce—really just puréed, roasted red bell peppers and seasonings—can be presented with cooked shrimp, toasted corn tortillas, or pita chips for easy dipping. It takes only minutes to prepare. For added convenience, you can substitute good-quality roasted red peppers from a jar. SEE THE RECIPES

QUESADILLAS AND GUACAMOLE

BELOW: Always keep a few avocados around so they will be ripe whenever you need a quick appetizer (they may be either too hard to use or too soft on the day you buy them), and store some flour tortillas in the freezer. In a few steps, you can make guacamole to serve with these white-cheddar-and-tomato quesadillas or toasted tortilla chips.

SEE THE RECIPES

DEVILED EGGS

ABOVE: Once a staple of picnics and family reunions, deviled eggs seem to have fallen out of vogue at some point along the way. These modern variations—served on a bed of daikon sprouts—offer tasty alternatives to the old mayonnaise-and-paprika standby. Start with a dozen freshly boiled eggs, and dress up the fillings with (above, left to right) crème fraîche (a light-tasting stand-in for mayonnaise), basil pesto, and spicy curry powder.

SEE THE RECIPES

HORS D'OEUVRE OPTIONS

The fun of hors d'oeuvres— literally "outside the meal"— is that there are no set rules for what you can serve.

While some hosts like to foreshadow flavors that will be part of the main course, you may prefer to serve hors d'oeuvres that are distinctly different from it. Hors d'oeuvres offer a chance to be creative, to highlight your skills with a particular cuisine or dish.

A fast hors d'oeuvre that can be put out in no time is endive leaves filled with crème fraîche, smoked fish such as tuna or trout, and a little dill. In the summer, I keep store-bought hummus in the refrigerator with a selection of cheeses; these can be quickly arranged on a platter with breadsticks, crackers, and raw vegetables. In the winter, I keep piped, ready-to-bake gougères, along with little phyllo pastries, in the freezer, which can be popped into the oven frozen.

Depending on the formality of the event, and whether or not you have help in the kitchen, composed hors d'oeuvres can be put together beforehand or offered in parts. The arrange-your-own approach means that each bite is a bit fresher and every texture more pronounced than when everything is preassembled. Best of all, guests get to make the hors d'oeuvres just the way they like them. —s.s.

CROSTINI TOPPINGS

Thin slices of baguette, a long French loaf, are brushed with olive oil and toasted to make crostini, one of the fundamentals of any hors d'oeuvre assortment. The toast is an excellent base that can be paired with a variety of homemade toppings. We've chosen three that are very different from one another; all are equally delicious: chickpea pimiento, olive tapenade and goat cheese, and tuna niçoise.

SEE THE RECIPES

WILD-MUSHROOM BRUSCHETTA This elegantly displayed hors d'oeuvre leaves the assembly to the guests. Toasted slices of rustic bread are topped with a mixture of chanterelle, porcini, and oyster mushrooms sautéed with garlic and white wine. The toasts are brushed with olive oil and stacked on a serving tray; a bowl of the mushroom mixture and a plate of garlic cloves are placed alongside. Serving the hors d'oeuvre unassembled saves time for the host and gives guests the option of rubbing garlic over their bread before choosing the amount of mushroom topping they prefer. SEE THE RECIPES

No. 3

LIGHTING

Lighting is an essential part of entertaining: It illuminates the setting, creates a distinctive mood, and casts an enchanting glow over guests and details alike. The right combination is equal parts practicality and aesthetics—and finding the proper mix is surprisingly easy. First, consider the space; whether guests will be seated or milling about; if you will be serving indoors or outside. Then, take a creative approach to your presentation. Look to the projects on these pages to guide and inspire you. Some, such as paper lanterns, you need make only once—stored properly, they can be put to good use again and again. Other ideas are as effortless as placing votives in terra-cotta pots or floating candles in bowls of water. Remember, too, that sometimes the simplest ideas are also the brightest.

OPPOSITE: *When transformed into candles, the shells you collected last summer can serve as lovely reminders of the beach. Deep shells, such as scallops and clams, make candles that burn longest. For how-to, see page 32.*

SHELL CANDLES

MATERIALS: *shells, bleach, paraffin wax or candle remnants, double boiler or two pots (one should fit inside the other), scissors, wicking, metal wick holder.*

To make the candles shown on page 30, first clean shells in a weak solution of bleach and water; let dry. Melt paraffin wax or candle remnants in the top of a double boiler (one with a lip is easier to pour from). Cut 2 to 3 inches of wicking, and attach one end to a wick holder. Pour melted wax into shell, then place the wick and holder in bottom of shell (do so carefully—wax is hot). If wick droops, trim it until it stands upright. Let wax cool until thoroughly hardened, about 30 minutes. The top layer of the wax hardens first, and the wax underneath will spill if it is not cooled completely.

PLEATED LANTERNS

MATERIALS: *varying sizes and colors of paper bags, utility knife, ruler, bone folder, ⅛-inch hole punch, round rayon cord (two 15-inch pieces per bag), candles, candleholders.*

A few folds turn paper bags into lanterns that shed soft light on a dinner table. With narrow luminarias like these, it's important for safety reasons to use candleholders that are three times as tall as the candles—or substitute battery-operated lights. **1.** Lay bag flat with bottom panel face up; fold bottom panel in half back onto itself (as shown in background), revealing crease. With utility knife and ruler, cut off bottom of bag along crease. Cut off top to create a straight edge. At each side, fold the top layer of the bag back onto itself, and crease new folds. Turn bag over, and repeat. **2.** Reverse all inward folds to make them outward folds, and crease them; there will be 10 outward folds in all. **3.** Bring two adjacent outward folds together; place one on top of the other, and crease the new interior fold. Repeat all around bag, creating 10 interior folds. Now you have an accordion-folded tube. **4.** Lay bag flat. With the point of bone folder, score across center of bag, perpendicular to folds. Flip bag over; score other side. **5.** Refold bag along accordion folds. Punch a hole in center of each panel at one end, ⅝ inch in from cut edge. Repeat on other end of bag. With bag folded, starting inside, thread a 15-inch piece of cord through holes on one end of bag. Adjust so opening is just large enough to slide candleholder through; tie on inside to secure. **6.** Put hand through untied end of bag; using one or two fingers, gently press outward along scored line in center. Lace cord through holes in other end, and tie as before. Set holder, with candle, on the table, and light before carefully setting lantern over it.

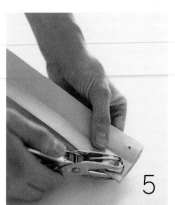

AUTUMN LIGHTS A perfect way to showcase fall's splendor, small glass cylinders are placed inside larger ones to create display "windows" for oak leaves and stalks of wheat. Ivory pillar candles complete the golden arrangement, which winds down the center of a long table. Select dried (not pressed) leaves that are slightly curled. These curved surfaces will help brace the leaves between the walls of the cylinders; flat pressed leaves would fall to the bottoms. Snip stems from leaves, and cut dried wheat heads, leaving $1/8$-inch stem. Drop stalks and leaves into the gap between the cylinders, making sure no part of them extends over the rim of the smaller cylinder (for safety reasons). Use a skewer to straighten stalks and leaves.

LEAFY LUMINARIA

MATERIALS: *ruler, waxed paper, scissors, skeleton leaves, glue stick, glass cylinder.*

Delicate skeleton leaves, available at crafts stores and floral-supply shops, set under waxed paper adorn inexpensive cylindrical candle-holders; the paper mutes the candlelight, casting an ethereal glow over the table. Cut a sheet of waxed paper slightly longer than the circumference of the cylinder so that the ends overlap slightly. Mount leaves to the underside of the paper by dabbing them with glue, being careful not to apply too much. Run glue along both ends of paper; affix one end to glass, wrap paper around candleholder, and press the overlapping portion to seal. If desired, scatter more leaves on the table, and cover the table with a sheer fabric overlay.

LEAF MOTH

MATERIALS: *4 skeleton leaves, hot-glue gun, delicate twig, candle wax, candleholder.*

Moths formed from filmy skeleton leaves in natural tones make elegant decorations to place through-out the house. Find two pairs of leaves that are as symmetrical as possible; one pair will become the top halves of the wings and the other pair the bottom. Begin on the top: Gently crease a leaf along its spine, and dab hot glue on its base; press base onto twig, angling leaf upward. Crease one of the bottom leaves, and dab base with glue. Attach where upper leaf meets twig; angle downward, letting leaves overlap slightly. Repeat on opposite side. Use a small ball of slightly melted candle wax to perch moth on a candleholder.

Glassine, rice paper, and tissue paper can transform plain votive holders or glasses into alluring candle shades. Place them around the house, use them to line a mantel or hallway, or group a few together on tabletops.

PAPER-AND-TWINE VOTIVES

ABOVE: Make a few matching votive holders from the same paper, or choose complementary colors and patterns for a varied arrangement. Glasses with smooth sides work best. Roll a piece of glassine paper around each glass, and trim the paper so the top edge extends beyond the top of the glass. Secure the paper with a bit of tape, and, if desired, cover with a smaller piece of glassine in a contrasting color. Tie with waxed twine; remove the tape. As an alternative, substitute two sheets of textured rice paper for the glassine and press leaves between the sheets. Insert tea lights or votive candles. OPPOSITE: Votive candleholders wrapped in tissue paper and twine are clustered among an assortment of pears on an octagonal footed cake stand.

SANDBOX SETTING

Tall, slender candles, staked in a sand-filled clay planter, preside over an informal table. Place one arrangement in the middle of a round table or line several down the center of a long rectangular one. Fill a pot with sand, and push the candles in deep. For a shallow container, anchors may be required to keep the candles in place: Set candles in $1/2$- or 1-inch floral frogs, and place them in the pot before filling it with sand.

MIRRORED VOTIVES

Votive candles are the perfect scale for an intimate dinner setting, dotting the table with soft pools of light. Here, a dozen white votives in clear glass holders are reflected in a framed mirror used as a tray. (The mottled glass of an antique mirror makes an intriguing platform.) To complete the composition, mix in two or three small glass vases brimming with flowers; trim the stems so the blooms sit just above the rims of the vases.

CITRUS AND FLOATERS

This centerpiece of floating candles and citrus slices is particularly enchanting for an evening celebration, because the candlelight flickers on the water. Slice lemons, limes, and oranges, and arrange them around floaters—in a range of colors that complement one another as well as the fruit—in a large glass bowl three-quarters full of water. Leave just enough room for the candles and fruit slices to gently bump against each other.

CANDLELIGHT

An important element in creating atmosphere, candlelight flatters everything— and everyone—it illuminates.

Candles can be the only light in a room or they can supplement electric lighting, which should be kept low when entertaining. Bear in mind that what may seem too dim at first will likely look perfect once your eyes adjust.

It takes time to light a room properly, so I always take care of this task well ahead of a party. If using glass votive holders, I make sure any leftover wax is cleaned out before replacing with fresh candles. (After a candle burns down, put the votive holder in the freezer until the wax is frozen. The wax will then pop right out for easy cleaning.) I put stands under pillars to catch dripping wax, and check that fresh tapers are fitted firmly into candlesticks and all wicks are trimmed and ready to light. Then I load a tray with candles so I can easily walk around to place them throughout the rooms. I often ask an early-arriving guest to help light the candles. If I'm having an outdoor party that starts during daylight hours and continues into dusk, I light whatever lanterns, torches, or candles I'm using before the natural light begins to fade, ensuring a smooth transition to evening. —S.S.

Soft-colored candles with a sparkling coating of sand befit an evening by the sea. We placed the candles, made from tinted beeswax, in candy dishes of varying heights and added a vase full of rugosa roses to the table.

OPPOSITE: ## A LINE
OF LANTERNS

OPPOSITE: At a Scandinavian-
inspired celebration of the summer
solstice, blue-and-white place set-
tings use the colors of the Finnish
flag. Oil lanterns with metal frames
that match this color scheme line
the center of the table, providing
rustic illumination when the sun
sets late in the evening.

SAND CANDLES

MATERIALS: *beeswax bricks, double boiler or two pots (one should fit inside the other), candy thermometer, candle dye, wooden spoon, wooden craft stick, sand, pail or other container, bottles or glasses for molds, number-4 square braided 100-percent cotton wick, scissors, pencil, paintbrush.*

1. Place beeswax in the top of a double boiler or in a lipped pan over a larger pot of simmering water (1-pound wax brick will yield a 4-inch-tall, 3-inch-wide pillar candle). Heat wax until a candy thermometer registers 175°F for a light dusting of sand, and up to 190°F for a thick sand crust.
2. Add about ⅛ of a square cake of candle dye (or multiple colors totaling that much) per pound of wax. Blend with wooden spoon. To test the color, dip a wooden craft stick into the wax; remove, and let dry (the finished candle will be slightly darker than the test-stick sample). Add more dye in small pieces until wax reaches desired color. **3.** Combine sand with water, using your hands, until it packs firmly enough to hold an imprint. Cover the bottom of a pail or other container with several inches of damp sand. Dig a hole in the sand, and place the mold in the hole, pushing it into the sand. Tightly pack additional sand around the mold to a height that equals the desired height of your candle, making sure it stays upright.
4. Hold mold firmly, and carefully ease it straight up and out of the sand. If the sand walls crumble, mix in a little more water and try again.
5. Cut the wick several inches longer than the candle, and dip the entire wick in melted wax to stiffen; let dry. Use a pencil to make a 2-inch-deep hole, centered, in the bottom of the mold. Place one end of the wick in the hole, and bury it using the pencil. **6.** Making sure the wick stays upright and centered, pour the wax in a slow, steady stream into the sand. Don't pour too fast, or the wax might cause the mold to lose its shape. Wax cools quickly, so if you're making more than one candle, return the wax to heat between pours. **7.** Let the candle set overnight, and remove it from the sand.
8. Dust off excess sand with a paintbrush, and use scissors to cut off the excess wick and wax at the base. On windy days, you might want to place the candles in glass hurricanes or other attractive enclosures.

WALL LANTERNS After sunset in this sheltered pergola, a mix of votive and pillar candles in various sizes, along with electric lights overhead, combine to give the impression of warm, natural light. Simple votive candles cased in metal lanterns are tucked amid the foliage of climbing ivy. Other votives in clear glass holders dot the tabletop; taller pillar candles illuminate the bar. Twin beams in the ceiling hide small low-voltage down lights, while up lights in each corner wash a "wall" of clipped arborvitae.

CAN LANTERNS

MATERIALS: *cans, masking tape, nails, hammer, 16-gauge wire, votive candles.*

Aluminum cans destined for the recycling bin are easily transformed into charming lanterns that can be hung from tree branches on a summer evening. Peel labels from cans, fill cans with water, and freeze overnight; the ice helps the cans retain their shape. On a 2-inch-wide strip of masking tape, sketch a design that's easy to repeat. Wrap the tape around the can. Following your pattern, lightly pound nails—small or large, depending on the hole size you desire—through the can. Form wire into a handle, bending both ends into a U shape. Use nails to make two additional holes, one across from the other under the top rim of the can. After the ice has melted enough to remove from can, push ends of handle through holes to attach, and insert a votive.

TERRA-COTTA VOTIVES

MATERIALS: *terra-cotta flower-pots, silver acrylic paint, paintbrush, votive candles.*

Terra-cotta pots, already at home in the garden, make any table setting shine when used to house votive candles. Metallic paint on the inside of the pot reflects the candle's flame. The 3-inch pots shown here are ideal to hold standard votive candles, although any size will work. Brush paint on the inside and top rim of a pot (left). Let dry, and place a votive inside.

HANGING COLORED-PAPER LANTERNS

MATERIALS: *pencil, styrene, colored paper, scissors, straightedge, bone folder, quick-drying glue, bulldog clips, hole punch, wire hooks, string of carnival lights.*

These fanciful shades are constructed by applying paper to sheets of styrene (the self-adhesive, pliable, paperlike plastic from which indoor lampshades are constructed). You can choose any colorful or patterned paper you like; we used two contrasting tones of art paper. **1.** To make a lantern with either a star-point or a cogwheel pattern, lightly trace the appropriate template (see Templates, page 138) with pencil onto an adequately sized rectangle of styrene, with the covered adhesive side down. Remove the peel, and press styrene onto a sheet of paper of the same size. **2.** Cut out along the pencil tracing. **3.** Hold a straightedge across the base of each star-point or cogwheel cutout. Run a bone folder along the straightedge to make a crease. Bend up the points or tabs evenly. **4.** Roll the shade into an open-topped cone shape, lining up the edges. Secure the seam with all-purpose, quick-drying glue and a bulldog clip until dry. Repeat all steps up to this point to make another shade. Join the two shades, wide bottom end to end: To make a star-point shade, align the points; glue the points together, and secure with bulldog clips until dry, about an hour. **5.** To make a cogwheel shape, press the tabs into alternating spaces to lock together without glue. Punch two holes across from each other at the top of each paper shade. Slip simple wire hooks through the holes and attach the shade to a string of carnival lights, aligning lights with shades. Keep in mind that styrene is not completely heat-proof; use bulbs no more powerful than 25 watts each, and provide for 2 to 3 inches of clearance on all sides of the bulb.

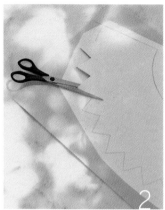

Multicolored paper lanterns, easily attached to a string of lights, make a wonderful outdoor alternative to candles. Woven through the branches of a tree, the lanterns seem magically suspended as they bob in the breeze.

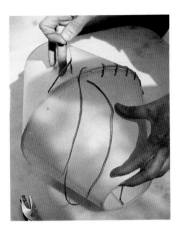

WIRE-AND-PAPER COLUMNS

MATERIALS: *wire-mesh sheeting, wire cutters, needle-nose pliers, rice paper, acrylic matte medium, paintbrush.*

LEFT: A trail of wire columns wrapped in rice paper softly lights a walkway. **1.** Cut an 18-by-21-inch sheet of mesh; when formed, the column will be approximately 6 inches in diameter. Holding a short side of the sheet toward you, cut away one horizontal side of each square, two rows deep, leaving the vertical edges intact. With needle-nose pliers, bend sharp ends of vertical exposed wires into small loops to form feet. **2.** Cut away outer edge of each square along one vertical edge; form remaining wire into hooks for securing column to itself. Form wire sheet into a cylinder, and use pliers to latch sides together using wire hooks.

3. Cut a rectangle of rice paper to cover column, excluding feet. Mix two parts acrylic matte medium to one part water; holding paper to column, apply matte-medium mixture liberally to paper with brush, soaking thoroughly so it will adhere to wire; use brush to push paper gently into grid work of column.

4. Stand column upright; let dry before inserting candle.

SEWN SHADES

MATERIALS: *pairs of lampshades, hole punch, upholsterer's (half-round) needle, soutache (fabric cord), lightbulbs, electrical cord.*

OPPOSITE: Standard lampshades, paired in size and shape and sewn edge to edge, can be suspended from a ceiling as lightweight carriage lanterns. They are lit with standard bulb sockets on electrical cords hung inside each pair of shades. A silk tassel adds an exotic note. Choose two identical harp shades; vary the colors if you like. With a 1/8-inch hole punch, make a row of evenly spaced holes, close to the wider, bottom edge of each shade. With upholsterer's needle and soutache, lace the shades together (above). To join two or more pairs of sewn shades, match small ends and thread them together through the crosspieces. Each pair of shades will require one lightbulb; suspend the bulb from a standard electrical cord that has a socket on one end and a plug on the other. Center a bulb between each pair of shades.

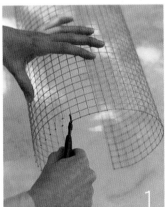

Carriage lanterns have more than simply decorative appeal. They are also quite practical, shedding steady light over a table, a garden, a porch. When choosing the materials with which to make them, consider color, texture, and translucence.

No. 4

FLOWERS & CENTERPIECES

———

The centerpieces we choose—whether bunches of flowers, festive paper pinwheels, or perfectly ripe produce—are what bring the table to life. To create something your guests will appreciate, be inventive and resourceful, and don't worry about making a grand statement. Flowers are the most popular choice, and working with them is not as difficult as it may seem. Select your favorites from whatever suits the season. Other elements, such as paper crafts, fruits, vegetables, and breads, add to the spirit of the party and the meal. Arrange flowers and centerpieces in traditional containers or explore other vessels. Center a large arrangement on the table, line smaller ones down the middle, or set a tiny display at each setting so guests can take home a reminder of the occasion.

OPPOSITE: *A white pumpkin is transformed into a homemade vase. Select a pumpkin about eight inches in diameter; cut off the top, and scoop out pulp and seeds. Place a small container, such as a highball glass, inside the pumpkin. Trim flowers to fit (we used twelve dahlias, but two dozen carnations would also work), and arrange in the glass.*

FLOATING
BLOSSOMS

OPPOSITE: Vintage finger bowls, teacups, and a champagne coupe are perfectly sized to hold single floating ranunculus blooms. Three ranunculus float in a larger pink bowl (top). The pink hues of the containers softly contrast with the crisp white flowers and tablecloth.
LEFT: Silver-plate bowls look regal when filled with pink lilies. Trim the stems so that the blossoms rest just below the rim of the bowl and some petals overlap it.
BELOW: On an outdoor table, full-blown roses float in a rough-hewn wooden bowl. Floral floaters help keep heavy blooms from sinking.

CONDITIONING FLOWERS

Giving cut flowers the right care can significantly extend their vase life. Here are six tips to help you get the most out of your arrangements.

1 *Fill your sink with cool water and submerge each stem as you re-cut it to desired length, at least one inch from the bottom, at a forty-five-degree angle.*

2 *Pull off any leaves or foliage that will fall under the water line. Submerged leaves rot and can contribute to bacteria and algae growth in the water.*

3 *If you want flowers to open quickly, place them in full sunlight.*

4 *Floral preservative, available at florists' shops, will help flowers last longer, giving them nutrients and making water easier to absorb. For a homemade solution, add one teaspoon each sugar and vinegar and one-quarter teaspoon bleach to a quart of water; alternatively, combine three cups water, one cup lemon-lime soda, and one-quarter teaspoon bleach.*

5 *Replace the water in a vase every day with cold water. If the water looks cloudy, pour it out and re-cut the stems before replacing the water.*

6 *To revive limp flowers, submerge them horizontally in a bath of cool water, covering the stems with a towel. They will absorb water through their pores, which will help plump them up.*

EGGCUP VASES

ABOVE: Gardeners cherish celestial blue forget-me-nots for the color they bring to beds and borders. But many floral designers dismiss them as too small to work with. The secret to displaying them is to look to your kitchen cupboard: Eggcups, demitasse cups, and cordial glasses are perfectly suited to their scale. Gather a generous bunch of flowers and strip away their leaves before arranging.

EGG-STAND CENTERPIECES

An antique French wirework egg stand becomes the centerpiece of a wicker table set for a springtime brunch. Lily-of-the-valley, grape hyacinth, and lady's mantle are placed in small terra-cotta pots on the stand's bottom tiers (the pots are painted with white or pale blue acrylic). A mixed arrangement on top contains all three flowers. For an Easter celebration, the lower tiers of the stand could be used to hold colored eggs.

JULEP-CUP NOSEGAY

A few red tulips accent a mix of orange tulips and ranunculus. We placed the flowers, with their petals still tightly closed, in a vintage mint-julep cup, though any short container can be used for a bouquet like this. To accommodate a full bunch, position shorter flowers around the perimeter of the cup and taller ones in the center. Low arrangements won't obstruct anyone's view, allowing guests to easily see and speak with others.

SHORT AND SWEET

In various shades of pink, from sultry fuchsia to soft baby pink, these short-stemmed bouquets of ranunculus and anemones are clustered in small drinking glasses and lined up in a row. We used about ten flowers for each small glass. Almost any flower will work for a similar display; simply cut the stems short enough for the blooms to form a dense but luxurious mound just above the rim of the glass.

LONG-STEMMED BUNDLES

Snowy puffs of paperwhites show off their clean lines in a row of footed crystal vases. The simple technique used to arrange them highlights the elegance of long-stemmed flowers, creating the illusion of a single, fluted green stalk crowned by a lush ball of blossoms. To create, tie tall stems with strands of raffia about an inch from the stems' bottoms and also just below the blooms, then fill vases almost halfway with water.

A MIX OF DAFFODILS

Five varieties of daffodils—'Dutch Master,' 'Grand Soleil d'Or,' 'Dick Wilden,' 'Sarah,' and 'Johann Strauss'—are joined to form a grand bouquet. Begin with three large blooms held in the crook of your hand. Continue adding flowers, circling the center at graduated heights, to create the domelike bunch. A clear footed vase emphasizes the smooth stems, which were cut to fit and twisted slightly before being set in place.

SINGLE STEMS

BELOW: This centerpiece of slender bottles—each holding a stem of white snapdragon, sweet pea, freesia, Amazon lily, or hellebore—can be pulled apart and transformed into favors. Fill bottles of varying heights with water, and add a drop of food coloring for a hint of translucent color (we used red). OPPOSITE: The cupped petals of these Oriental poppies look lovely on their own. Before arranging in small glasses, singe cut ends of stems with a lighted match to give them a longer life.

A single-stemmed arrangement can often have as much visual impact as an elaborate bouquet. Instead of traditional vases, look for bottles, juice glasses, and inkwells to emphasize the grace of an individual flower.

VINE AND CLEMATIS CENTERPIECE This long tabletop display of white *Clematis* 'Caroline,' mauve *Passiflora* 'Star of Bristol,' and *Passiflora caerulea*, with its dark corona, was inspired by the floral cascade on an outdoor trellis. The blossoms will last only one day, so cut them just before mealtime. This arrangement can be made with almost any cut flowers, and ivy works as well as the clematis vine shown. Weave the vine among the containers, tucking the cut ends into a bowl.

HANGING CENTERPIECE

LEFT: A centerpiece composed of two planters hangs above an open-air table setting—high enough so as not to obstruct guests' views but low enough so that they can appreciate the ornamental foliage. The verdigris copper buckets were filled with containers of gold-leafed sweet potato (*Ipomoea batatas* 'Margarita') and lily turf (*Ophiopogon*) and suspended by planter chains from hooks screwed into a rafter.

REFLECTING-POOL CENTERPIECE

RIGHT: Blossoms of floating clematis could almost be mistaken for a reflection of the flowers above them. Arrange two bunches of clematis flowers, stems, and leaves in a tall cylinder. Place the arrangement in the center of a wider, shallow cylinder filled less than halfway with water. Snip additional flowers from their stems, and float them in the "pool."

THE PICK
OF THE GARDEN

RIGHT: Even gardeners who love
fresh vegetables often overlook
their decorative potential. Here,
cherry tomatoes add a splash of
red to soft arrangements of lark-
spur, scabiosa, hydrangea, and
daisylike feverfew set in ironstone
jars. Floral waxed paper and
checked ribbon help transform the
centerpieces into nosegays; for
farm-stand-worthy party favors,
set one bouquet atop a wooden
produce basket packed with ripe
tomatoes and trimmed with ribbon.

ANEMONES
AND RADISHES

OPPOSITE: On this large table, cartons and jars filled with radishes—
foliage intact—and bunches of
bold red anemones make casual
but striking adornments for an outdoor setting. Striped tea towels
used as napkins match the palette.

PAIL CACHEPOTS

LEFT: Free from gritty sand, beach
buckets are pleasing to the eye,
with their sturdy proportions and
bold colors. We put them to decorative use as cachepots. A few pails
of simple arrangements, such as
the daisies shown here, make an
easy summer centerpiece.

Fanciful fans like these let you experiment with prints and colors. Use varying designs and sizes of paper for a few, and solids in complementary colors for others. Set one on each place, and gather several for an interesting centerpiece.

FIREWORKS FANS

MATERIALS: *paper, stapler, scissors, craft glue, paintbrush, paper clip, thin wood strips such as coffee stirrers, colored twine (optional).*
Making these fans takes little more effort than wielding them for refreshment on a warm day. You can create them in just about any size: Our largest fans are eight inches across, while the small swizzle-stick toppers are only three inches from tip to tip. **1.** Begin with a sheet of paper as wide as you want your fan to be and about 1½ times as long. Starting on a short side, accordion-fold the paper. **2.** Staple the folded paper in the center, with the staple perpendicular to the folds. Cut a curved profile at each end. **3.** Splay the fan so that open edges of one side meet. Lay a thin line of craft glue along these edges. Press glued edges together, and secure with a paper clip until the glue dries. You will now have a partially opened fan. Glue a wood strip to each side of the remaining open sides. If you want to keep the fan open permanently, tie the handle sticks together with colored twine.

LEMON CENTERPIECE

LEFT: This colorful centerpiece not only looks lovely, it also fills the dining room with a fresh scent. Meyer lemons are piled high in a large shallow bowl. Then chamomile flowers with their bright golden stamens—and a few lemon leaves—are tucked into the gaps between the fruits. The vivid yellow of the lemons brings out the paler gold of the tablecloth.

HARVEST BUCKETS

OPPOSITE: Wooden baskets are filled with peaches, nectarines, and Gala apples. At the table's center, one shallow basket is upended to make a pedestal for another. The bottom halves of the baskets are stuffed with kraft paper, and the fruits are arranged in pyramids on top.

FALL COMPOTE

RIGHT: A trip to the market inspired this informal composition of kumquats, winter squash, and an orange bell pepper in a ceramic compote. While the ingredients for this particular display are available only during the colder months, you can adapt it any time, using seasonal fruits and vegetables.

For any edible centerpiece, choose foods you truly want guests to eat: Fruits should be at their ripest; breads baked from a favorite recipe. Be sure to set out plenty of extras so the display won't look sparse as guests help themselves.

EDIBLE CENTERPIECES OPPOSITE: Oversize breadsticks in celery glasses arranged down the center of the table make delicious decorations. They alternate with pillar candles and ornamental berry branches, which, along with the ribbon napkin ties, introduce bright color to an otherwise neutral palette. ABOVE: We stacked silver cake stands to create a graduated display of warm potato rolls, but glass, porcelain, or ceramic stands or footed compotes would work as well.

No. 5

TABLE COVERINGS

You and your guests are likely to spend much of your time gathered around the dinner table, so it makes sense to dress it well. It is possible to make that surface inviting, comfortable, and functional—protected from hot dishes that may cause damage—with little effort and a few everyday items, spruced up for the occasion. Begin from the bottom with the tablecloth, but don't stop there. Consider how runners, placemats, and trivets will work with your entertaining style and the meal at hand. Decorative pieces can be elegant or whimsical, spirited or charmingly subdued. Choose themes, colors, and materials that relate to the season, the surroundings, or the pattern of the dinnerware. Most important is that your guests feel drawn to the table, and comfortable throughout the meal.

OPPOSITE: *Autumn leaves displayed beneath a sheer tablecloth bring the brilliance of the season indoors. Place leaves between paper towels or waxed paper inside a telephone directory for about a week to smooth. If needed, use double-sided tape to affix foliage to a solid white tablecloth; lay sheer cloth, such as the pale-yellow chiffon shown, on top.*

EATING OUTDOORS

A few simple measures will help keep some forces of nature under control and make alfresco dining even more enjoyable.

TABLES *Be creative when choosing what to use, whether it's folding card tables or sawhorses. A decorative covering can give almost any table a festive look.*

WEIGHTING *When eating outside, it's wise to prepare for wind. Fishing-line weights are small and heavy, and take only a minute to sew onto the nearly invisible line, which can then be sewn around the edge of the tablecloth. This keeps the edges of the cloth from flopping over. You can also use clips as anchors, attached to the edges or corners of the table, or weight the cloth with attractive shells or rocks.*

NETTING *If you're setting an outdoor table ahead of time, you can drape mosquito netting over the entire table to keep bugs and drifting blossoms or leaves off the plates. The filmy netting looks romantic, so you may want to leave it over the table after guests arrive until you're ready to eat.*

DISHWARE *Don't overlook the possibility of bringing indoor tableware outside. It feels delightfully indulgent to drink from nice wineglasses while out on the lawn. Even if you're using a picnic table, the setting can be elegant if you add pretty linens and silver utensils.* —S.S.

BANDANNA TABLECLOTH

MATERIALS: *3 different pairs of bandannas, needle, thread.*
On the range, cowboy bandannas did duty as everything from food sacks to hats, and also served as placemats. These bandanna tablecloths probably won't travel farther than a backyard picnic. To make, lay a matching pair of bandannas face to face, and stitch together along one side, 1/2 inch from edge. Unfold. Repeat with two remaining pairs, forming three panels. Lay two panels face to face, and stitch them together along one long side, 1/2 inch from the edge; attach the third panel the same way.

STRIPED RUNNER An outdoor lobster dinner is casual by nature; these striped table runners make the event feel festive, too. At this picnic table in the Maine woods, the ticking pattern on the fabric whimsically echoes the stripes of the lobster bibs set at each place. Placemats in a complementary orange act as individual runners, spilling over the picnic table at each seat. Rocks chosen for their smooth, round shapes hold the runner in place on a windy day.

FOLIAGE RUNNER A table covering need not be made of fabric. Unusual greenery provides an interesting backdrop, especially for a buffet with platters and bowls full of colorful foods. On this table in a Miami garden, a striking runner for traditional Cuban dishes has been made from loosely woven strips of swordlike leaves (cattails or palm leaflets work well). Serving pieces are arranged directly on top of the weave and interspersed with orchids floating in small ceramic bowls.

WOVEN-MAT TABLECLOTH

MATERIALS: *straw placemats, sewing machine fitted with standard needle and thread, ½-inch grosgrain ribbon.*

This woven-straw tablecloth makes any meal feel like a picnic on the beach. You will need four straw placemats. **1.** Stitch together a pair of placemats along the short sides, using a zigzag stitch. Topstitch a length of grosgrain ribbon over the seam. Repeat with the second pair of mats. **2.** Sew the pairs together along the long edges; stitch from the center out to prevent bunching. Topstitch another grosgrain ribbon in place to cover the length of the seam. Finish all four sides of the resulting tablecloth by topstitching with grosgrain ribbon around the outer edge.

A stylish tabletop should be keyed to the tone of the occasion.
For this springtime lunch at a farmhouse, the lightweight texture of a burlap
tablecloth feels perfectly suited to its bright, airy surroundings.

BURLAP TABLECLOTH

Burlap, cut from a bolt purchased at a fabric store or garden-supply center, is a casual covering for any dining table—and it's as inexpensive as it is chic (shown on pages 76 and 77). Just roll the fabric over a table to the desired length, then cut to fit. This material is also eco-friendly: After the meal it can be recycled as mulch for your garden.

FELT RUNNER

MATERIALS: *wool felt, fabric scissors, needle and thread, iron, pinking shears.*

Add a swath of warmth and color to a snow-white tablecloth with a two-toned runner. The runner should be 3 inches shorter than the table-cloth at either end. Cut each of 2 pieces of wool felt in complementary colors to a length that equals half the length of the runner plus 1 inch, and a width of 18 inches. Sew pieces together at short ends, leaving a 1-inch seam allowance; iron seam flat. Trim perimeter of runner with pinking shears. Finish by top-stitching in contrasting thread $1/2$ inch from edge all around.

LEAF RUNNER MATERIALS: *oak leaves, paper towels, telephone directory, ¾- to 1½-inch grosgrain ribbon, iron, needle and thread, acorns, hot-glue gun, small preserved oak leaves (available from floral-supply stores).* Oak leaves, so abundant in the fall, can make natural, brocadelike table runners when dried. We glued them to grosgrain ribbons cut to size, and weighted them with acorns. To make, collect oak leaves two weeks in advance, and lay them between sheets of paper towels to press. Place paper towels with leaves between the pages of a telephone directory; replace paper towels every few days. Decide length of finished runner; cut ribbon 1 inch longer than measurement. Fold ends over ½ inch, and iron flat. Fold in corners at ends to form a point, and iron flat. Sew three stitches along the seam; add an acorn by wrapping thread around stem and threading into point (right). Hot-glue dried oak leaves onto ribbon. For a colorful effect, alternate dried oak leaves with the preserved oak leaves as you go.

Use fresh foliage to create simple fabric designs. Green and pliant leaves, especially leathery ones, such as those of the magnolia tree, make the best prints. Palm, anthurium, ruscus, eucalyptus, lemon, and bay leaves are also effective.

LEAF-PRINT TABLECLOTHS

MATERIALS: *sponge brush, fabric paint or textile-screening ink, leaves, cloth, paper towels, rubber brayer, iron.*

Use untreated fabrics, like linen and cotton, which will absorb the paint or ink. Fabric paints and textile-screening inks come in a narrow range of colors, but you can mix them to subtle effect. Use fabric paint, which is more opaque, when working on dark-colored fabrics. The tablecloth shown at right is bedecked with lemon leaves in shades of blue. A round cotton tablecloth (opposite) was printed with monstera leaves in something close to their natural color. When designing a leaf print, first experiment with patterns and color schemes on fabric remnants. When using one color, it is appealing to overprint the same leaf shape in slightly different densities; let the paint or ink dry before printing the second layer. **1.** Since stems tend to shift during this project, print leaves and stems separately, starting with leaves. With a sponge

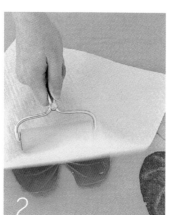

brush, paint the underside of a flattened leaf (these are anthurium); aim for the thinnest yet thorough coat to produce a detailed image. Turn leaf over, and place it on the fabric. **2.** Cover leaf with a paper towel, and roll over it several times with a brayer. **3.** Lift leaf gently from its tip, pulling straight up. For variety, use both sides of leaves in prints—the underside will show the veins more clearly. When you are finished printing and paint has dried, heat-set all paints with an iron, following the paint manufacturer's instructions.

SNOWFLAKE FRILLS MATERIALS: *tissue paper, rotary cutter, heavy card stock, scissors, pencil, utility knife, hole punch, paper tablecloth, cake stand, tape.* Paper tablecloths aren't just for children's parties. Along with cake frills, they dress up a holiday dessert table. For the tablecloth, begin with a sheet of tissue paper large enough to cover the table. Fold it lengthwise into strips, like a fan, making strips slightly wider than the snowflake template. Fold the resulting long, folded strip of paper in half so the short ends meet. Trim edge of paper with a rotary cutter to create a scalloped border. Trace template (see Templates, page 138) onto heavy card stock, and cut out. Place template over tissue paper. With a pencil, trace the pattern onto the paper near the scalloped edge; cut out design with a utility knife and a hole punch through each fold. Unfold, and place over a paper tablecloth. For cake frill, measure circumference of cake stand; cut a 3½-inch-wide strip of tissue paper to that length. Fold widthwise into 2-inch fanlike pleats, and follow directions for table edging. Create a zigzag edge with scissors; tape frill to cake stand.

HOLIDAY TRIMMINGS

In a season filled with the sound of bells, jingle bells provide an appropriate tablecloth accent. Linen cloths with an openwork hem are widely available—and easy to embellish. Cut four pieces of silk ribbon as long as each side of the tablecloth. Weave one ribbon through the ladder-like holes on each side, and tie a jingle bell to the overhang of each ribbon.

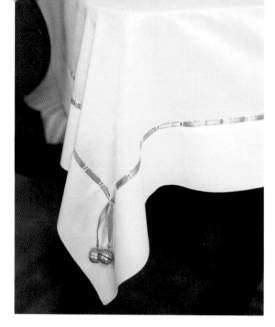

SNOWFLAKE TABLECLOTH

MATERIALS: *pencil, loose-leaf paper, organza tablecloth, craft glue with fine-tip applicator, silver glitter.*

To capture the sparkle of snowflakes, re-create them in glitter on an organza overlay. Begin by creating templates: Using a pencil, draw flakes, between 2 and 8 inches wide, on sheets of lined paper. Slide template under tablecloth; trace lines onto tablecloth using craft glue (below). Remove template. Sprinkle glue with silver glitter. Let dry; shake off excess glitter. Craft glue is water soluble, so cloth should not be washed once it has been decorated.

ROLLED PLACEMATS

MATERIALS: *bamboo mat, ¼-inch-wide grosgrain ribbon, napkin, utensils.*
Bundled with napkin and utensils in one roll, these placemats are great for backyard barbecues or buffets. Begin with a 12-by-18-inch mat and 18 inches of ribbon. Thread ribbon from beneath mat, between first and second bamboo strips from right edge (leaving 6 inches extending over edge). Thread ribbon back under mat and then up again about 1 inch farther from edge of mat. Loop around knife handle; pass through mat. Secure fork and folded napkin in the same manner, leaving an inch in between. Roll up mat from left. Tie ribbon bow around roll, and trim neatly.

REVERSE-PAINTED GLASS TRIVETS

MATERIALS: *¼-inch glass squares (cut and polished by a glass shop), clean cloths, oil-based paint, paintbrush, masking tape or frisket film (available at art-supply stores), single-edge blade, craft scissors, felt, craft glue.*
Painted glass trivets brighten any meal, such as an afternoon tea (opposite). The ³/₄-inch-thick glass adds a sense of texture to an otherwise flat surface. Prepare glass by cleaning it thoroughly on all sides (clean surface to be painted last, to avoid fingerprints). A single solid color works best on smaller squares. Paint back of glass with two coats of oil-based paint, letting the paint dry completely after each coat. (Use a clean cloth to wipe away any excess along edges before paint dries.) On larger squares, create a patchwork of colors. We chose five subtly different shades of blues, greens, and white. Use masking tape or frisket film to tape off a grid on the back of the glass. Apply two coats of each color; remove tape, and clean edges of painted squares with the single-edge blade. When paint is completely dry, apply tape again, leaving previously taped sections bare, and paint the remaining sections. When entire surface is dry, cut felt with craft scissors to fit bottom of each trivet; brush glue over paint, and press felt into glue. Trim excess felt from edges.

LINEN TRIVETS

MATERIALS: *2 or 3 pieces of thin bulletin-board cork (available at stationers), matching linen napkins, craft glue, needle and thread.*

Protect a dinner table without sacrificing formality by turning pairs of linen napkins into slipcovers for cork trivets. Measure and cut pieces of cork to fit inside a set of linen napkins. Glue cork layers together. Sew napkins together along three sides, keeping stitches close to the edge; slide cork into open side. Remove cork after dinner, and launder the napkins.

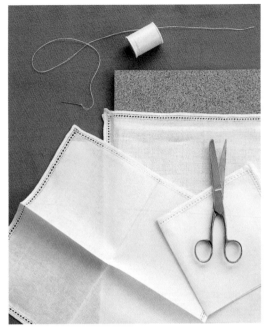

STEEL TRIVETS

MATERIALS: *stainless steel, thin bulletin-board cork, utility knife, silicone adhesive, plastic knife, paper towel (optional).*

Because steel conducts heat, you'll need to back this trivet with cork (if you intend to set extremely hot items on it, use two layers). Have a kitchen-supply company or sheet-metal fabricator cut a piece of stainless steel to desired size. Clean the back well. Place the steel on top of a piece of cork, and use a utility knife to cut cork to desired size. Apply a bead of silicone adhesive or sealant around the edge of steel back; make cross of adhesive from corner to corner. Spread adhesive using plastic knife. Place the cork on the steel, and press; turn trivet over and weight it with heavy books while adhesive sets. If adhesive oozes from the sides, wipe it away with a paper towel.

WOOD-PLANK TRIVET

MATERIALS: *4-foot-long section of 2-by-12 Douglas fir, 1-inch-square wood strips, wood glue, wire brush, alkyd high-gloss enamel paint, cloths (for rubbing in stain), maple-color wood stain, paint thinner.*

Trim edges of plank to make them even and square. To form feet, use wood glue to affix 1-inch-square strips to the bottom of the plank. The feet should be recessed 1 inch from the sides (we used 4 feet for our trivet). To give the top surface of the wood an appearance of age, go over it with a wire brush. Then paint the edges, feet, and underside (skipping the top for now) with enamel paint. When the paint dries, begin finishing the top of the plank by dabbing a cloth in wood stain and rubbing it into the grain. (Rubbing stain in gives a softer color finish than brushing it on.) Once the stain dries, dab a clean cloth into thinner and then into the enamel, and rub the paint into the surface. When dry, this final coat will give the plank the depth of a waxed finish; it will also enhance the color of the stain.

No. 6

NAPKINS

Though there are some rules of etiquette associated with napkins—for example, dinner napkins should be twenty inches square or larger—when it comes to easy entertaining, a little creative license is not only granted but welcome. While they are essential tools for keeping tidy, napkins can also be transformed into decorative details that grace the table. Stylish presentation involves a bit of artistry, but it's easily mastered. Fold them, roll them, embellish them, tie them, clip them, even tuck them into empty glasses. Just be sure to practice your technique and make up a bunch early on, especially if you're expecting a crowd. And remember, it's really only an initial impression you are after, since all too soon, your rolled or folded creations will be unfurled as they are put to work.

OPPOSITE: *Also called the water lily or the artichoke, this lotus-flower napkin fold is one of the best-known napkin arrangements and will be familiar to anyone who ever made a paper "fortune-teller" as a child. For how-to, see page 98.*

FERN NAPKINS

MATERIALS: *heavy paper stock, cotton or linen napkins, fern fronds, tape, hammer.*

These linen cocktail napkins were inspired by John Mickel, a curator of ferns at the New York Botanical Garden, in New York City, who wears a laboratory coat patterned with images of ferns. **1.** Place a sheet of heavy paper stock on a smooth work surface. Top with a napkin, and then a fern frond or two, taping fern lightly in place. Cover with another piece of paper. **2.** Hold down top piece of paper, and hammer firmly. The pounding will release the leaf's chlorophyll into the fabric, creating the image. Follow the lines of the fern rather than pounding randomly. Ironing and washing will not harm the image, but with time, or exposure to the sun, the color will fade to an attractive brown.

STONE WEIGHT

A coral-colored napkin is loosely folded to achieve a ripple effect, then centered on a plate and anchored with a stone found on the beach. Look for medium-size stones that will complement a napkin fold, not overpower it; thoroughly clean stones with soap and water, and let dry before using. This table is set for a dinner party featuring the flavors of India, where exuberant color combinations—such as those used in the arrangement of roses and candles—are common. The overall effect, however, is balanced by the simplicity of the dinnerware, utensils, and glasses.

BREAD RINGS

These heart-shaped napkin rings are not just pretty—they are also edible. To make the shapes, roll a strip of store-bought pizza dough between your hands to form a rope. Onto a parchment-lined baking sheet, drape rope into a heart shape, with loose ends of dough meeting at top. At the bottom of the heart, make a curl (as shown below). Join the two ends at the top of the heart by gently pinching the dough together with your thumb and forefinger. Bake in a 400°F oven until hearts are crisp and golden, about 20 minutes. Let rings cool before rolling napkins into loose tubes, then weaving each through a bread ring (right).

COOKIE-CUTTER NAPKIN RING

Create your own collection of napkin holders with a set of cookie cutters. We used stars for a Fourth of July party; other shapes lend themselves to other occasions. Roll up napkins, and slip one through each cutter (right). The cutters can also double as useful party favors for guests to take home with them.

PAPER LEAVES

MATERIALS: *green craft paper, glue, paper-covered wire (available at crafts stores), napkins, ribbon.*

For evergreen napkin holders, which are always in season, use paper leaves. Trace or draw a leaf, and use it as a template to make more from craft paper. Glue a leaf to each end of a piece of paper-covered wire long enough to loop around a rolled napkin (see center of far right photo). Once dry, center napkin atop wire; twist the leaves together, encircling the napkin. Tie ribbon into a knot at base of leaves to finish.

STAR-ANISE
NAPKIN HOLDERS

MATERIALS: *suede cord or thin decorative ribbon, star-anise pods, hot-glue gun, napkins, scissors.*
These pretty fasteners are functional and fragrant: Star-anise pods secured to lengths of suede cord keep rolled napkins in place and release a subtle scent. Thread a length of cord long enough to wrap around the rolled napkin plus a few inches of overlap under the stiff stem of a spice pod; if there is no stem, dab hot glue on the back of the pod and press it onto the center of cord. Roll napkins, position star anise in front, and tie cord in back. Trim excess cord.

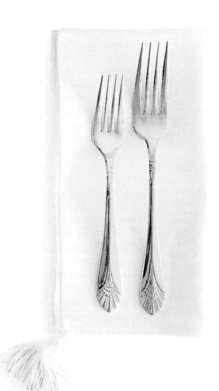

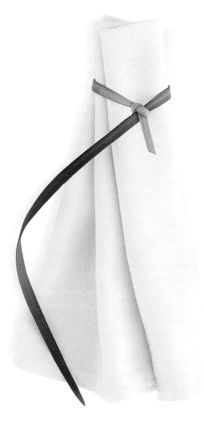

BUTTON LOOP

Fold a napkin in half from top to bottom and then from side to side. Roll loosely; pull ends to skew. Form a loop in one end of a 5-inch length of elastic cord, and knot. Thread other end through a two-hole button; knot. Wrap around napkin; fasten loop around button.

TASSEL

Lightly handstitch a 2-inch tassel, available at trimmings or notions stores, to the corner of a napkin. Position the napkin so the tassel is at the bottom right; fold napkin in half from top to bottom and then in thirds from side to side, folding the left side in first.

LEMONGRASS TIE

Accordion-fold a napkin. Wrap a fresh stalk of lemongrass around the top of the napkin. Knot stalk near one end, letting the other end hang down the length of the napkin. Pull ends of napkin to skew slightly. Raffia or hemp fiber can be used in place of lemongrass.

Any simply folded napkin can be embellished, with wonderful results. And it doesn't take a lot of time or money, especially when you make use of common notions or household items, such as extra buttons, tassels, or ribbons.

CLOTHESPIN WRAP

Fold a napkin in half from top to bottom and then from left to right, to form a square. Place flatware on top of napkin, and pinch sides together to meet. Clip sides at the center with a white or colored miniature clothespin to hold flatware securely in place.

FLOWER BLOSSOM

Fold napkin in half from top to bottom, then left to right. Fold left side to center; fold right edge to overlap left. Turn so hem edges are at top. Slide utensils into pocket. Peel back top two corners so points meet fold; fold back next two to overlap. Press; set dahlia on top.

RIBBON TIE

Fold a napkin in half from top to bottom and then from right to left. Fold in thirds from side to side, folding left side first. Fold top-left corner of napkin under. Slip in utensils. Wrap striped grosgrain or other decorative ribbon around napkin, and knot in front.

ROSE NAPKIN

This display—tucked into a tumbler at each place setting at a dessert party—takes two square napkins to make: a green one for the leaves and the color of your choice for the rose. Form leaves first. Don't worry about making the corners meet perfectly—a little unevenness looks more natural. **1.** Fold the green napkin in half diagonally. **2.** Fold it in half again along long edge. **3.** Fold it once more in half along long edge. Set aside. **4.** To create flower, fold napkin in half diagonally. Place on work surface so that longest side of resulting triangle is at top. Fold up corner opposite longest side so that it just extends over top of long edge. The top and bottom edges should be parallel. **5.** Fold up bottom edge so that it falls just short of top edge. Begin rolling napkin from one side. Guide and adjust the cloth as you roll to give it a budlike shape. **6.** Slip completed flower between top and bottom halves of green napkin, and arrange in a glass.

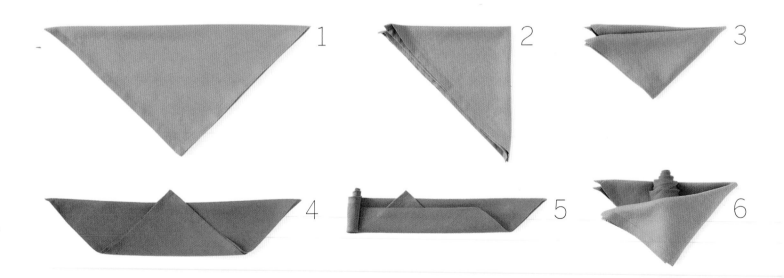

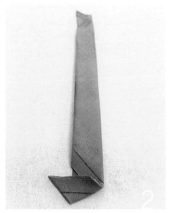

ROLL-UP NAPKIN

This napkin fold is easy to create, but your guests will never know. Start with clean, pressed linen or cotton napkins, and keep the iron hot, with sizing or starch handy. **1.** Start by folding the napkin in half diagonally to form a triangle, positioning the long folded edge on the left side. Fold the right points over to meet the middle of the left edge, and iron. Fold into thirds lengthwise, ironing creases at both folds. **2.** With the napkin folded along the creases so that it is long and flat, fold the bottom 1 to 2 inches of the napkin up and over to the left, creating a point on the left side. **3.** Holding the point down with one hand, use the other hand to tightly roll the napkin around the point, forming a fat cylinder. **4.** When you have finished rolling, tuck the tail of the napkin into the top or bottom of the roll. You may need to adjust the top point by pulling it up out of the cylinder or tucking it farther down into it. Place the napkins on top of whatever plates are set at the first course.

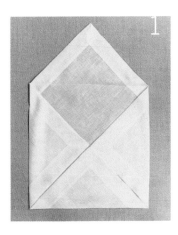

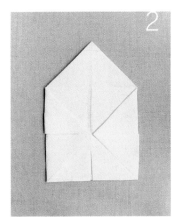

LOTUS-FLOWER FOLD To make this fold (shown completed on page 88), start with clean, pressed linen or cotton napkins, and keep the iron hot, with sizing or starch handy. **1.** Fold a dinner napkin in half diagonally, pressing to crease; open napkin, fold diagonally in the opposite direction, and crease. Continue to press all folds as you go. Open the napkin; fold all four corners to the center, creating a square. **2.** Flip the napkin over, and fold the corners back to meet at the center, forming a smaller square. **3.** Pressing down on the center of napkin, reach underneath and pull up the flap at each corner to create flower petals.

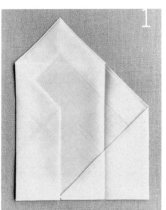

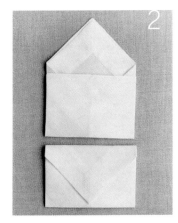

ENVELOPE FOLD

Elegant yet simple, this napkin fold sealed with a spoon looks especially appropriate at an informal meal or a tea party. Start with clean, pressed linen or cotton napkins, and keep the iron hot, with sizing or starch handy. **1.** Fold a napkin in half diagonally, letting the bottom edge show about ¹/₈ of an inch, and press the fold; press and starch all folds as you go. Fold in the two bottom corners of the resulting triangle so they meet at the center of the long edge. Then fold the sides over so they meet in the center. **2.** Fold up the bottom half to about ¹/₂ inch below the triangle flap. Fold flap down, closing envelope, and press to finish.

ROSE NAPKIN FOLD

This sculpted flower fold, favored by the venerable French chef Auguste Escoffier, is one of several used to present individual items of food at a meal. Fruit, such as the bunch of grapes shown at left, and dinner rolls are the usual choices. The napkin's contents should be clearly visible. Start with clean, pressed linen or cotton napkins, and keep the iron hot, with sizing or starch handy. **1.** Fold a dinner napkin in half diagonally, pressing to crease; open napkin, fold diagonally in the opposite direction, and crease. Continue to press all folds as you go. Open the napkin, and fold each of its four corners to the center, creating a square. **2.** Fold the four new corners of the napkin to the center, creating a smaller square. **3.** Repeat, folding in the corners to make an even smaller square. **4.** Flip the napkin over. Fold the four corners in to meet at the center of the square. **5.** Pressing down on the center of the napkin, reach underneath and pull up the flap at each corner to create flower petals. **6.** Pull the remaining corners from underneath into cupped petal shapes. Place the napkin on a plate, and tuck contents into the center.

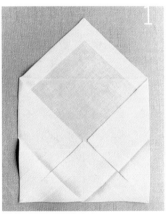

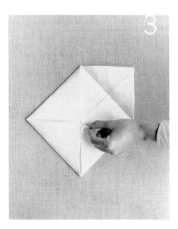

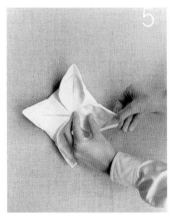

No. 7

PLACE CARDS

There is no more personal way to make a guest feel welcome than to reserve a place at the table, marked with his or her name. Whether they're classic white tented rectangles or colored paper cut into clever shapes, place cards are decorative as well as functional. They can be paired with simple or practical objects, such as miniature fruits, potted plants, or elements of the meal to come. You may handwrite the cards or print them on a computer. If the cards are not intended to be freestanding, use ribbons or stickpins to hold them in place. Once you've designed the cards, you'll have to decide where to put each one. Matching dinner partners can be a delicate task, but take comfort in knowing that the place cards themselves can stimulate congenial conversation among guests.

OPPOSITE: *Golden apples are the perfect accompaniment to place cards trimmed into the shape of leaves. Thin satin ribbon, tied around the apple's stem and through holes punched in the cards, attaches the leaves to the apple.*

WALNUT HOLDER

LEFT: The bumpy shell of a walnut is not as wobbly as it appears—with a bit of patience you can find the nut's balancing point. After locating this spot, cut a slit with a utility knife or small saw on the opposite side of the walnut (the side that will face the ceiling) and insert the place card, with name written on it, into the opening.

PUMPKIN PLACE CARDS

BELOW AND OPPOSITE: Miniature white pumpkins serve as place-card holders for a fall dinner. To attach the cards, make a small slit in the tip of the stem using a utility knife or small saw. The pumpkins, set in glazed bowls, mark each place setting; more pumpkins sit in terra-cotta pots and alongside white candles in the long dining table's center.

POMEGRANATE PLACE CARDS

ABOVE: Rosy pomegranates anchor the name tags and add a splash of color to a neutral place setting. Red toothpicks secure the paper-leaf cards to the fruits. The pomegranates are then set in soup bowls; they will be removed before the first course is served.

PAPER ROSES

A trio of rosettes and a leaf, all made of paper, adorn tented place cards inscribed with a child's best penmanship. To make, cut out a spiral template (see Templates, page 138). Roll paper from outermost edge. Dab glue on the flower's base to secure. Cut out leaf template, crease in half lengthwise, and glue to tented card; glue roses on top of leaf. As an added embellishment, float real roses in small glasses at each place.

LEMON SQUEEZE

Wrapped in cheesecloth, a lemon half serves as both condiment and place-card holder. When the lemon is squeezed for seasoning, the cheesecloth prevents squirting and catches wayward seeds. The cloth is secured at the lemon's base with a length of colorful silk ribbon; a scallop-edged card is hand-written and rimmed in color, then hole-punched and attached to the ribbon before the trimming is neatly tied into a bow.

BOUND NAPKIN

Attaching this place card to a napkin takes mere moments. Fold napkin in thirds. Using a hole punch, make a pair of holes in card; holes must be smaller than ribbon. Cut ribbon long enough to wrap around napkin twice. Snip ends at an angle; slip each into a hole from front. Pull taut; keeping one end short, wrap other end around napkin; even out ends. Thread each ribbon end through opposite hole from back; pull taut. Trim ends.

WHEN TO USE A PLACE CARD

While not every party requires formal seating arrangements, a seated dinner party does.

Even if you are having a buffet, you may wish to use place cards if your guests don't know one another very well. It can be awkward to approach a table of strangers, and many people will be relieved to have introductions at least partially made for them. It helps to have everyone turn the place cards around once they are seated, or you can make tented place cards with each guest's name inscribed on both sides.

When planning your seating arrangements, think about how the conversation will likely flow. When you're hosting various groups of people, or several couples, it's a good idea to break up those who are already acquainted. People will often stick to those they know unless they are given an opportunity to mingle with those they don't.

To help keep the conversation lively, place your more gregarious guests near the center of the table rather than at an end. Seat a shy guest next to someone who is likely to coax him out of his shell. After all, the main reason to use place cards is to help everyone have a wonderful time. —S.S.

PAPER IRIS

MATERIALS: *purple and green craft paper, scissors, pencil, glue, bone folder.*

Definitely not your garden-variety place cards, these paper flowers are nevertheless pretty for a garden party. Using templates (see Templates, page 138), trace shapes onto paper (use purple for flower and green for leaves and stem); cut out. Curl every other petal downward by wrapping each around a pencil. Lift remaining petals; glue together at tips, overlapping slightly. For stem: With a bone folder, score the paper lengthwise down the middle; make a 1/2-inch cut along fold at one end. Fold over stem and glue up to slit. Bend sections outward to form two tabs. Glue top of tabs to bottom of flower; let dry. Write guest's name on one leaf. Glue this and another leaf to stem base, overlapping slightly.

FALLEN LEAVES

The silhouette of autumn leaves is re-created in cut paper. Two halves of a leaf form a whole where the interlocking ends of a napkin ring meet. The matching place card is crowned by a smaller example of the same leaf. Use templates (see Templates, page 138) to cut out construction-paper napkin ring; cut the two slits along axis of leaf. Roll up ring so slits interlock. Cut out place card. Cut out half leaf shape with a utility knife. Fold card along dotted line so half of leaf stands up.

POTTED ORCHIDS Potted green, white, and ruby *Paphiopedilum* orchids decorate a luncheon table at Martha's home in Westport, Connecticut. An arrangement of three orchids of varying heights serves as a centerpiece, while single plants hold place cards and double as favors for the guests. The terra-cotta pots and saucers were gilded with silver leaf; additional silver-gilded saucers hold white candles that surround the centerpiece. Hand-written place cards are slipped into wire stands staked in the plants' dirt. This place-card idea works with any small potted plant or floral arrangement.

No. 8

DESSERTS

The finale is the most eagerly anticipated part of many meals. Delight your guests with treats as scrumptious to look at as they are to eat, but let it be your secret that they're not at all hard to make. The key lies in having the right ingredients close at hand. A kitchen stocked with supplies, such as fine-quality baking chocolate and unsalted butter, as well as the freshest fruits of the season, enables you to whip up something satisfying at a moment's notice. It is also wise to keep a few staples, such as homemade pastry doughs, dessert toppings, and slice-and-bake cookie dough, in your freezer, along with cartons of favorite ice creams and a box or two of puff pastry. With some basics—and just a little bit of effort—you can give your guests a deliciously sweet send-off.

OPPOSITE: *Ice cream is a natural choice for summer desserts. For this architectural presentation, let a pint of ice cream sit at room temperature for a few minutes. Gently ease ice cream from its container by running a thin knife or spatula around the edge of the pint, then upend it on a serving plate. Top with berries, mint leaves, or other garnish.*

HOMEMADE DESSERTS

A delicious homemade dessert is a sure way to wow guests, and there's no reason it has to be elaborate or fussy.

Most of us have been in the habit of saving room for dessert since childhood. It's often the part of a meal we remember best. Keep that in mind whenever you entertain, and try to offer something at least partially made from scratch.

Warm desserts can cause people to go weak in the knees. A warm fruit crisp is always a hit, and requires very little in the way of baking experience or know-how. I like crisps made with apples or pears in the colder months and rhubarb, berries, or stone fruits in the spring and summer. They are even more delectable served with vanilla ice cream.

I've never heard a complaint about ice cream, no matter what the season. Toppings such as chocolate, caramel, and fruit sauces are quick to prepare, and if you also have cookie dough or baked cake layers in your freezer, you have all the components of a wonderful dessert. Serve slices of butter cake topped with ice cream and fruit purée, or cookies with ice cream and berries or sautéed fruit. Use your imagination, and you'll always be able to give guests a dessert worth remembering. —S.S.

COFFEE ICE CREAM AFFOGATO

The word *affogato* means "drowned" in Italian; affogato al caffè is a popular dessert in which hot espresso is poured over gelato just before it is eaten. Although traditional gelato is denser than ice cream and therefore melts more slowly, you can use either one for equally sumptuous results. If you prefer, substitute very strong brewed coffee for the espresso.

SEE THE RECIPES

CHOCOLATE MINI-CAKES

Single-serving cakes are a fine alternative to slices of a full-size 8- or 9-inch round. They make serving simple, since there's no need to cut and plate each piece. These chocolate minis are baked in jumbo muffin tins; coating the tins with butter and sugar gives the cakes sparkle and a bit of crunch. Their sunken centers make an ideal bowl for a scoop of ice cream.

SEE THE RECIPES

PEPPERMINT HOT-FUDGE SUNDAES

Hot fudge may be an old-time favorite, but here's a twist that even traditionalists will find hard to resist: The topping is flavored with peppermint extract, available at most supermarkets. Pour the fudge over vanilla ice cream scooped into a clear, tall glass for a mouth-watering presentation. The peppermint is a refreshing counterpoint to the fudge and melds well with the creamy vanilla. Coarsely chopped peppermint candies strengthen the taste and add a delightfully crunchy texture to this nostalgic dessert.

SEE THE RECIPES

CHOCOLATE-CHIP
SKILLET COOKIE

Our giant cookie is soft, sweet, and
filled with a combination of semisweet and milk-chocolate chips.
The dough is pressed into a skillet (below, left), then baked until
golden brown. To dress it up, make
a creamy caramel topping (below,
center). Serve a warm wedge of
cookie topped with vanilla ice cream
and the sauce (below, right).

SEE THE RECIPES

ESPRESSO BISCUITS

Mix two favorite desserts, cookies and ice cream, with a flavor that is appropriate for the end of a meal: coffee. Serve espresso biscuits alongside coffee ice cream in café-au-lait bowls—the vintage ones shown here were bought at a flea market. The dense flavor and crisp texture of the rich biscuits complement the lighter taste and creaminess of the ice cream.

SEE THE RECIPES

RASPBERRY ANGEL FOOD CAKE

BELOW: It's beaten egg whites—there are no yolks or butter—that make angel food cake light enough to float away. In our version, fresh raspberries are puréed and added to the cake batter, lending just the right amount of tartness and color to bring everything back down to earth. SEE THE RECIPES

CHEWY ORANGE-ALMOND COOKIES

OPPOSITE: A combination of fruit and nuts gives these cookies their unique flavor. Orange zest and ground almonds are baked right into the batter (it's important to weigh the nuts for accurate amounts, since volume can differ enormously). Additional almond slivers make a fitting garnish. SEE THE RECIPES

BANANA PILLOWS Sometimes store-bought can be as good as homemade, especially when you're pressed for time or kitchen space. Frozen puff pastry is sold in most supermarkets; it usually comes in folded sheets. When making these "pillows," cut dough along the folds to help prevent uneven rising. Bake the pastry until golden, then cut a pocket from each top and fill with velvety banana cream. Chocolate curls make a delicate garnish whose flavor complements the banana filling. SEE THE RECIPES

BITE-SIZE TARTLETS

Miniature tart shells make sweet serving dishes. A coconut crust is baked in tiny brioche or tartlet tins, then filled with vanilla-flavored whipped cream and topped with crystallized ginger. Alternatively, you can fill the tartlets with lemon or lime curd. Fresh berries or cherries also make a nice topping.

SEE THE RECIPES

MARSALA CHEESE TART WITH ORANGES

This rich and creamy cheesecake is far easier to prepare than most; it requires no baking. The ginger-snap crust is pressed into place, then the delectable filling is simply spooned on top and frozen until firm. The cream cheese gets its sweetness from vanilla and a bit of Marsala—a sweet Italian wine used to flavor such dessert sauces as zabaglione. Just before serving, garnish the tart with sectioned oranges.

SEE THE RECIPES

EASY MELON SORBET

LEFT: This refreshing frozen dessert requires no ice-cream maker, just fresh melons and a food processor. First cube melons—use a variety, such as watermelon, honeydew, and cantaloupe, for the most colorful presentation—and freeze in resealable storage bags. Place frozen cubes one at a time in the food processor, and purée. Add water if necessary to smooth. Add sugar to taste, and purée again. Serve immediately, or freeze in an airtight container up to 2 weeks.

FROZEN GRAPES

Fresh grapes are a delight on any table but tend to wilt on hot, humid days. Freezing seedless grapes not only revives them, but turns them into a cooling treat as well. Rinse grapes under running water and pat dry. Place on a tray and freeze for 2 hours or until firm. If served immediately, grapes will be tangy and firm. Even if they defrost a bit and lose some of their firmness, they'll still be luscious.

MELON SALAD

Cutting open a melon and scooping
out its fragrant flesh is one of the
great pleasures of summer. Drizzled
with ginger-infused syrup and garnished with mint and orange zest,
slices of cantaloupe and balls of
honeydew and canary melon will
keep everyone cool on a swelter-
ing afternoon. Orange lace cookies
are a crisp accompaniment.

SEE THE RECIPES

No. 9

TIPS & TECHNIQUES

Seasoned hosts know that in order to entertain successfully, you need to rely on a few tricks. Time-saving techniques and easy cleanup ideas help make hosting more treat than task, but most valuable of all are methods that help keep you organized. Having everything in order well before guests arrive creates a more relaxed and comfortable atmosphere. Chopping and measuring all ingredients in advance allows you to cook more neatly and efficiently. Pre-setting tables and choosing serving pieces for each component of the meal takes the last-minute rush out of presentation. Even tending to tedious details—before and after a party—such as pressing linens, trimming candlewicks, and removing wine stains promptly, will make you all the more prepared to entertain again soon.

OPPOSITE: *When deciding on which dishes to use, set out an assortment of pieces to determine which go best with the food being served as well as with the rest of your table setting. Place a slip of paper on each, noting its assigned role, and add the proper utensils. The labels will assist any host's helpers in carrying out the plans, too.*

PLACE SETTING

BELOW: Even for casual table set-tings, you'll want to put everything in its proper place. Align the bottom of flatware with the bottom rim of the dinner plate. The water glass goes directly above the knife, whose blade always faces inward, while the wineglass is placed to the right, above the spoon. When it's time to serve dessert and coffee, clear away all but the water glass and spoon, to make room for clean plates, flatware, and cups.

IRONING A MONOGRAM

RIGHT: To keep an embroidered design or monogram crisp and clear, iron it facedown against a towel. The soft texture of the towel will prevent the embroidery from get-ting flattened. Finish by turning the cloth right side up and ironing gently around the design. Starch also helps keep shape: You can use spray starch, or for extra crispness, add liquid or powder starch to the rinse cycle of your wash.

WATER GLASS

KNIFE

WINEGLASS

DINNER FORK

SALAD FORK

NAPKIN

SPOON

SALAD PLATE

DINNER PLATE

STAIN FIRST-AID KIT

Have emergency supplies ready so you can take immediate action on stains at your party. Blotting is the first line of defense. Use white cloths, white paper towels, or sponges. Liquid spills on carpets can be lifted more easily if you flush them out with soda water. If there is still residue after blotting, a healthy sprinkling of baking soda should draw it out. For a red-wine spill, a splash of white wine will do the trick. On linens, a generous amount of salt minimizes red-wine stains before they dry.

POST-PARTY STAIN REMOVAL

Fear of red-wine stains probably keeps more fine linens on the shelf than on the table. Here's a surefire, easy way to get rid of red-wine stains that have had time to dry: Wet the stain with lukewarm water, then add a layer of table salt. Rub salt in; let it sit for five minutes. Pull the stained section of the fabric taut across a heat-proof bowl, and secure with a rubber band. Place in the sink, and carefully pour boiling water on the stain from a height of about three feet. The pressure and heat of the water will eliminate the stain.

AFTER-DINNER CLEANUP

Cleaning up can be made easier if you have a good strategy in place. These tips will have your kitchen back in working order in record time.

1 DISHES *Starches, such as flour and oats, and dairy products, such as milk and eggs, get gummier in hot water. Use cold for dishes with these ingredients, and hot for all others. Soak dishes for a few minutes, as bacteria can grow quickly.*

2 POTS AND PANS *To loosen cooked-on food, fill the bottom of the pan with water, and bring it to a boil on the top of the stove. After a few minutes, the pan can be scraped clean with ease.*

3 SCRAPS BOWL *Keep a stainless-steel bowl beside the sink to collect fruit and vegetable scraps, tea bags, eggshells, coffee grounds, and so on. Then make a single trip to the garbage can or outside to the compost heap.*

4 GREASE *Never put cooking grease down the drain: Animal fats cause the fats in soap to congeal, eventually clogging your drainpipe. Pour grease off into a lidded container before discarding.*

5 GARBAGE DISPOSAL *Deodorize and sharpen the blades of an in-sink disposal with vinegar-and-water ice cubes. Alternatively, grind citrus peels while flooding the disposal with boiling water. Vinegar will neutralize some odors, and citrus is an effective air freshener.*

CUTTING STEMS

Take a measured approach when cutting stems so that flower arrangements always look their best. Dip a plastic ruler at an angle into the base of whatever container you'll use (far left), and note the height at which you'd like the blossoms to rest. For arrangements with blooms at varying heights, note more than one height at once. Then dry the ruler, and set it flat on your work surface. Lay flowers one at a time on the ruler, and snip the stem at the desired length with floral shears or a sharp knife (left).

FLORAL-TAPE GRID A grid of floral tape provides firmer support than a conventional frog, and more control over the placement of each flower. (Alternatively, you can use transparent tape with a shallow glass bowl.) Attach strips of tape across the top of the bowl at ½-inch intervals in one direction; repeat with tape strips laid at right angles to the first set of strips. Fill the bowl with water. Before trimming each flower stem, hold it up to the container to determine how much to cut. For a low arrangement like this, the tallest stems should be about twice as long as the container is deep. Holding each stem under water, cut its end at a 45-degree angle. Remove any foliage that would fall below the water line in the container. Insert the stems into the tape grid, starting with the larger blooms and filling in with the smaller ones. Position flowers at the rim so their petals conceal the tape.

 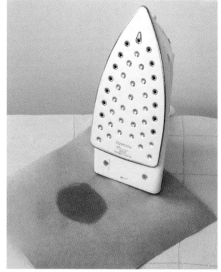 

CANDLE TIPS A little care goes a long way toward keeping candles burning brighter, cleaner, and longer. ABOVE LEFT: Avoid black smoke by trimming wicks to ¼ inch before lighting. After snuffing flame, probe wax gently with a spoon handle to center the wick, to prevent uneven melting and drips. ABOVE CENTER: Scrape spilled wax off linens with a dull knife. Put several layers of kraft paper under linen and one sheet on top of stain. Iron on low until wax is drawn into paper. ABOVE RIGHT: Clean drips on tables by blow-drying hardened wax on low for several seconds, then scrape away wax with the edge of a credit card; wipe residue.

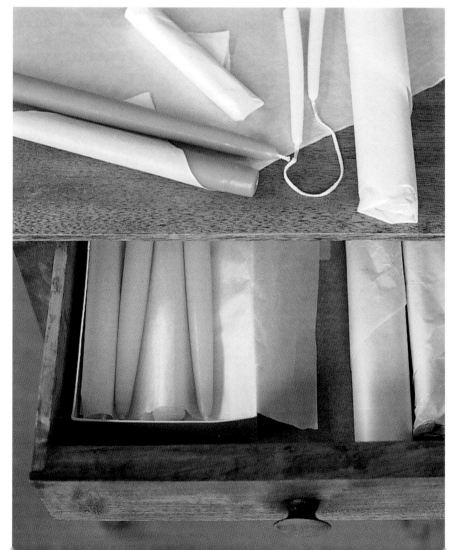

STORING CANDLES

Tapers are beautiful, and though they are delicate, they can last through multiple uses if tended to properly. Pack candles flat in paper-lined drawers or boxes to protect them from scratches and breakage. Keep sets together by wrapping them in tissue paper before putting them away. If you have an extensive collection, consider affixing a label to the outside of the tissue to identify color, fragrance, and size.

A HEAD START Our favorite approach to cooking comes from the kitchens of France and can be adapted to any recipe. *Mise en place*, as the French call it, is the practice of having all of a dish's ingredients prepared and ready to combine—measured, chopped, diced, or sliced according to recipe instructions before you begin. Place each in a clear glass bowl to make identification easy. Set aside in an unused corner of work space, or refrigerate as necessary. This trick is especially helpful when you are making a dish that needs to be served immediately after cooking, since it will minimize the time spent away from guests.

NATURAL AIR FRESHENER

LEFT: The strong odors of fish, fried foods, and some vegetables can overwhelm cooking and dining areas, detracting from the otherwise appetizing smells of a homemade meal. To rid the air of lingering aromas, simmer a half-dozen lemon slices and a handful of whole cloves in a pan of water for at least 10 minutes while you're cooking or cleaning up.

WARM ROLLS

BELOW: Your guests have been anticipating soft, warm dinner rolls from the moment the aroma first wafted from the oven. But by the time the basket is passed around the table, the rolls are often too cool even to melt butter. Keep them warm longer by putting a few clean, unglazed terra-cotta tiles in the oven for the last 5 minutes of baking. Using potholders, place the hot tiles in a towel-lined basket, add rolls, and cover.

SIFT LIST

ABOVE: If you've ever lost track of which dry ingredients you'd placed in a bowl for sifting, you know it can be hard to tell whether sugar or salt has been added to flour. Next time, hang a fine-mesh sieve over your mixing bowl, and place the most plentiful ingredient—say, flour—into the sifter first. Add the other ingredients on top, in visible mounds, and sift it all at once.

PRESCOOPED
ICE CREAM

BELOW: Rather than wrestle with a
container of unsoftened ice cream
while your eager guests wait for
dessert, prepare scoops ahead of
time. Cover a rimmed baking sheet
in plastic wrap for insulation, then
begin scooping. For the smoothest
spheres, dip ice-cream scoop in cool
water as you go. These single-dip
servings will hold their shape in the
freezer until you're ready to transfer them to bowls or cones.

FREEZER
SHORTCUTS

ABOVE: The prospect of making
dough from scratch on the day of
your party may be too daunting.
Instead, set aside an hour days or
weeks before to prepare a few
batches. Pâte brisée (above, bottom), French for short pastry, is a
flaky dough that freezes well and
can be used for both pies and
tarts. All you have to add is fresh
fruit filling. Topping (above, center)
for fruit crisps and the doughs for
various cookies (above, top right)
also keep well in the freezer.

SEE THE RECIPES

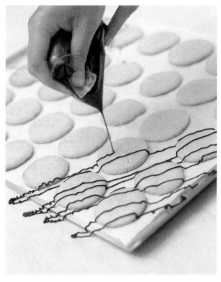

DECORATING COOKIES ABOVE: No technique is faster or easier than this. Cut chocolate into chunks (above, left), seal in a resealable freezer bag, and microwave on high until chocolate melts, 30 seconds to 1 1/2 minutes. Let stand until cool enough to handle. Arrange baked cookies on a parchment-lined baking sheet (above, center); the closer together they are, the less chocolate will be wasted. Use scissors to snip as small a hole as possible in a corner of the bag. Drizzle chocolate over cookies in stripes, spirals, even initials. Let chocolate set; transfer cookies to a serving plate (above, right), or refrigerate until ready to serve.

ICE-CREAM
TOPPINGS

LEFT: Stocking up on the essential ingredients for ice-cream sundaes means you're always ready for guests. Select an assortment of cones, and prepare easy-to-make chocolate fudge sauce and caramel sauce ahead of time. Both of these sauces can be refrigerated up to one week. Quickly cooking some berries with a little sugar makes a delicious and simple fruit sauce for sundaes, too.

SEE THE RECIPES

The Recipes

DRINKS

FROZEN BLOODY MARYS
SERVES 2

Allow time to freeze the tomato chunks. For yellow and orange Marys, use only one teaspoon of Worcestershire sauce. Instead of bottled juice, use a juice extractor to extract juice from orange and yellow tomatoes.

½ cup bottled red tomato juice
1 tablespoon freshly squeezed lemon juice
1 cup fresh tomato chunks, frozen
1 tablespoon plus 1 teaspoon
  Worcestershire sauce
3 dashes hot-pepper sauce
2 ounces vodka
¼ teaspoon salt
1½ cups small ice cubes
  Freshly ground black pepper
  Skewered small tomatoes, fresh basil, and
  cubed mozzarella, for garnish (optional)

Combine tomato juice, lemon juice, frozen tomatoes, Worcestershire sauce, hot-pepper sauce, vodka, salt, and ice in a blender; season with pepper. Process until smooth. Divide mixture between two glasses. Garnish with skewers, if using.

VIETNAMESE FRUIT SHAKE
MAKES ONE 2-CUP SHAKE

½ large ripe avocado, mango, or papaya,
  peeled, pitted, and cut into chunks
¼ cup sweetened condensed milk
2 cups ice
1 tablespoon sugar, plus more as-needed

Pulse ingredients in a blender or food processor until smooth. Add more sugar as desired.

PEACHMOPOLITAN
SERVES 1

3 tablespoons vodka
3 tablespoons peach schnapps
2 tablespoons peach nectar or juice
1 tablespoon freshly squeezed lemon juice
  Finely crushed ice
  Peach slice, for garnish

In a cocktail shaker, combine vodka, schnapps, peach nectar, and lemon juice with ice; shake mixture well. Strain into a martini glass, and garnish with peach slice.

LEMON MINT JULEPS
SERVES 10

To hasten the cooling of the sugar syrup, pour it into a bowl and place in an ice-water bath. Stir until cool, about five minutes.

2 lemons
1 cup sugar
1 cup water
1 cup packed mint sprigs, plus more
  for garnish
  Finely crushed ice
15 ounces best-quality Kentucky
  bourbon (2¼ cups)

1. Chill 10 small glasses or mint-julep cups. Using a sharp paring knife, remove all peel from lemons; set peel aside. Juice lemons; set aside.
2. In a small saucepan, combine sugar and the water, and bring to a boil. Add lemon peel, and simmer 2 minutes. Remove from heat; let stand until cool, about 45 minutes.
3. Place mint in a medium bowl; using a wooden spoon, press down on mint to crush leaves. Pour sugar syrup over leaves; let stand at room temperature 1 to 2 hours. Strain, discarding mint and peel. Add lemon juice to syrup; mix to combine.
4. Fill chilled glasses with enough crushed ice to slightly mound over the tops. Into each glass, pour 1½ ounces (3 tablespoons) bourbon and 2 tablespoons syrup. Stir well, and garnish with a mint sprig. Serve immediately.

MEYER LEMON DROP
SERVES 1

Meyer lemons are especially delicious, but any lemons will work for this recipe. You may substitute two teaspoons superfine sugar for the lemon syrup if desired.

Sugar, for rim of glass
Powdered yellow food coloring (optional)
Lemon slice
¼ cup vodka
2 tablespoons freshly squeezed Meyer
  or other lemon juice
1 tablespoon Lemon Syrup (recipe follows)
1 teaspoon Cointreau
  Finely crushed ice

Tint sugar with food coloring, if desired. Spread sugar in a saucer. Moisten rim of a martini glass with lemon slice; dip in sugar. In a cocktail shaker, combine vodka, lemon juice, lemon syrup, Cointreau, and ice; shake well. Strain into prepared glass; garnish with lemon slice.

LEMON SYRUP
MAKES ABOUT 1½ CUPS

1 cup sugar
1 cup water
  Grated zest of 1 lemon

In a small saucepan, combine sugar and the water, and bring to a boil over high heat. Add lemon zest, reduce to a simmer, and cook about 10 minutes. Remove from heat. Cover, and let stand overnight at room temperature. Store, refrigerated in an airtight container, up to 2 weeks.

PINK SALTY DOG
SERVES 1

Coarse salt, for rim of glass
Grapefruit slice
⅓ cup freshly squeezed pink grapefruit juice
2 tablespoons vodka
1 tablespoon Campari or grenadine
1 to 1½ cups ice cubes

Spread salt in a saucer. Moisten the rim of a martini glass with grapefruit slice; dip in salt. In a blender, combine juice, vodka, and Campari; blend. With motor running, add ice until slushy. Pour into glass; garnish with grapefruit slice.

CRANBERRY CIDER
MAKES 4 CUPS

1 orange
32 ounces cranberry juice
2 three-inch cinnamon sticks
1 two-inch piece fresh ginger,
  peeled and sliced
Sugar, to taste

With a vegetable peeler or a sharp knife, remove two 3-inch-long strips of peel from the orange; juice orange. In a medium stockpot, combine orange juice, orange peel, cranberry juice, cinnamon sticks, and ginger. Add sugar if desired. Bring mixture to a simmer over medium-high heat. Reduce heat to low, and simmer 20 minutes. Strain, and discard solids. Serve hot.

COFFEE WITH COGNAC AND CARDAMOM
SERVES 4

For best results, use strong coffee.

⅔ cup water
⅔ cup turbinado sugar
6 cardamom pods, lightly crushed
1½ cups heavy cream
⅔ cup Cognac or other brandy
2 cups plus 2 tablespoons freshly
  brewed coffee

1. In a medium saucepan over medium heat, bring the water, sugar, and cardamom to a simmer, stirring to dissolve sugar; turn off heat. (Syrup can be refrigerated in an airtight container up to 1 week. Before using, gently reheat.)
2. When ready to serve, whip cream to soft peaks. Add brandy and hot coffee to syrup in saucepan, and stir to combine. Divide among four glasses, and top each with a generous dollop of whipped cream. Serve immediately.

HORS D'OEUVRES

BACON-AND-ONION MINI QUICHES
MAKES 6 FOUR-INCH QUICHES

All-purpose flour, for work surface
Pâte Brisée (page 137)
6 strips bacon, cut into 1-inch pieces
2 onions (about 12 ounces),
  cut into small dice
3 ounces Gruyère cheese, grated (1½ cups)
½ cup milk
½ cup heavy cream
2 large whole eggs
1 large egg yolk
  Pinch of freshly grated nutmeg
  Coarse salt and freshly ground pepper

1. Place six 4-inch bottomless ring molds or tart pans on a parchment-lined baking sheet; set aside. On a lightly floured work surface, roll out one pâte brisée disk to slightly less than ⅛ inch thick. Cut out three 5½-inch rounds. Fit each round into a ring mold; prick bottom of dough all over with a fork. Repeat with remaining pâte brisée disk and ring molds. Freeze or refrigerate until well chilled, about 30 minutes.
2. Preheat oven to 375°F. Line each tart shell with parchment paper, leaving a 1-inch overhang; fill with dried beans or pie weights. Bake until edges are lightly golden, about 25 minutes, rotating sheet halfway through. Remove from oven; remove paper and weights.
3. Return to oven, and continue baking until centers of crusts are golden, about 8 minutes. Transfer to a wire rack to cool completely.
4. Meanwhile, cook bacon in a small skillet over medium heat until crisp and brown, about 8 minutes. Transfer to paper towels; let drain. Pour off all but 1 tablespoon fat from skillet. Add onions; cook over medium-low heat, stirring frequently, until golden brown, about 25 minutes. Combine onions and bacon in a small bowl.
5. Divide cheese evenly among prepared shells. Top with onion mixture. In a medium bowl, whisk together milk, cream, eggs, and yolk. Add nutmeg; season with salt and pepper. Divide evenly among shells, covering onion mixture.
6. Bake until quiches are set in the center, about 15 minutes. Transfer to a wire rack to cool, at least 10 minutes or up to several hours. Serve warm or at room temperature.

TOMATO-AND-OLIVE MINI QUICHES
MAKES 6 FOUR-INCH QUICHES

All-purpose flour, for work surface
Pâte Brisée (page 137)
3 ounces Gruyère cheese, grated (1½ cups)
9 cherry tomatoes, quartered
18 Niçoise olives (about 1 ounce),
  pitted and quartered
2 teaspoons finely chopped fresh
  flat-leaf parsley
½ cup milk
½ cup heavy cream
2 large whole eggs
1 large egg yolk
  Pinch of freshly grated nutmeg
  Coarse salt and freshly ground pepper

1. Follow recipe for Bacon-and-Onion Mini Quiches through step 3.
2. Divide cheese evenly among prepared shells. Arrange 6 tomato quarters on top of each, and sprinkle with 1½ teaspoons olives and ⅓ teaspoon parsley. In a medium bowl, whisk together milk, cream, eggs, and egg yolk. Add nutmeg; season with salt and pepper. Divide evenly among shells, covering cheese and other ingredients.
3. Bake until quiches are set in the center, 15 to 20 minutes. Transfer to a wire rack to cool, at least 10 minutes or up to several hours. Serve warm or at room temperature.

OLIVE TARTLETS
MAKES 50

All-purpose flour, for work surface
1 17¼-ounce package frozen store-bought
  puff pastry, thawed
10½ ounces goat cheese, room temperature
1 pound pitted mixed olives, such
  as Kalamata, Niçoise, or green
  Spanish, cut in half

Preheat oven to 375°F. Line 2 baking sheets with parchment paper. On a clean, lightly floured work surface, roll out pastry ⅛ inch thick. Using a 2-inch cookie cutter, cut out rounds; place on prepared baking sheets. Prick each several times with a fork; spread with 1 teaspoon goat cheese, and top with 3 or 4 olive halves. Bake until pastry is puffed and golden, about 25 minutes.

GOUGERES

MAKES ABOUT 8 DOZEN

Unbaked gougères can be frozen for up to one month; bake them just before serving.

1 cup plus 1 tablespoon water, plus more for dough if needed

½ cup (1 stick) unsalted butter

1 teaspoon salt

½ teaspoon cumin seeds, roughly chopped

1 cup all-purpose flour

5 to 6 large eggs

½ cup finely grated aged Manchego or Gruyère cheese

1. Preheat oven to 375°F. Line two baking sheets with parchment paper; set aside. Combine 1 cup water, butter, and salt in a medium saucepan. Bring to a boil over medium heat; cook until butter is melted. Remove from heat; add cumin and flour. Stir with a wooden spoon until combined. Return to medium heat; stir constantly until dough pulls away from sides and leaves a film on bottom of pan, 2 to 4 minutes. The dough should be smooth and should not stick to your fingers.

2. Transfer to the bowl of an electric mixer fitted with the paddle attachment; beat on medium speed until dough cools and stops releasing steam. With mixer on medium speed, add 4 eggs, one at a time, incorporating each completely. Dough should be shiny and a string should form when touched with your finger. If no string forms, lightly beat another egg, and add a little at a time. If a string still doesn't form, add water, 1 teaspoon at a time. Add cheese, and mix until combined.

3. Transfer batter to a pastry bag with a plain ¼-inch tip (Ateco #4). Pipe 1-inch mounds 2 inches apart on prepared baking sheets.

4. In a small bowl, whisk together remaining egg and tablespoon water; brush over mounds. Bake 20 to 25 minutes. Prop open oven door slightly with a wooden spoon; continue baking until mounds are golden on outside and slightly damp on insides (test by piercing one). Remove from oven. Serve warm or at room temperature.

CHEESE COINS WITH JALAPENO JELLY

MAKES ABOUT 6 DOZEN

2 cups all-purpose flour, plus more for work surface

1 teaspoon salt

1 teaspoon paprika

½ teaspoon cayenne pepper

1 cup (2 sticks) chilled unsalted butter, cut into small pieces

1 cup freshly grated sharp white cheddar cheese

⅓ cup jalapeño jelly

1. Combine flour, salt, and spices in a food processor fitted with the metal blade; pulse to combine. Add butter; pulse until mixture resembles coarse meal. Add cheese; process until dough starts to hold together.

2. Turn out dough onto a lightly floured surface; knead a few times. Divide into 4 equal pieces, and roll into logs, each about 6 inches long and 1¼ inches in diameter. Wrap in plastic; refrigerate until firm, at least 1 hour or up to 3 days. Dough can be frozen at this point up to 1 month.

3. Preheat oven to 350°F. Cut dough into ⅓-inch-thick rounds; place 2 inches apart on a parchment-lined baking sheet. Bake until lightly browned, about 20 minutes. Remove from oven; let cool on baking sheet 1 minute, then transfer to a wire rack to cool completely.

4. When ready to serve, spoon a small amount of jelly onto center of each coin.

GARDEN-HARVEST TEMPURA

SERVES 6

¾ cup plus 2 teaspoons cold water

1 large egg

¾ cup all-purpose flour

⅛ teaspoon baking soda

¼ teaspoon salt, plus more for sprinkling

1¼ pounds assorted vegetables, such as squash, string beans, eggplant, or carrots

3 cups vegetable oil

½ cup sesame oil

Large bowl of ice water

Tempura Dipping Sauce (recipe follows)

1. Place the cold water in a small bowl. Whisk in egg, flour, baking soda, and salt. Chill in the refrigerator 30 minutes.

2. Wash and trim all the vegetables; cut into small pieces, no more than 4 inches long and

½ inch thick. Cover with a damp paper towel, and refrigerate about 15 minutes.

3. Prepare an ice bath; set aside. In a medium saucepan, heat vegetable and sesame oils over medium-high heat until a deep-fry thermometer registers 375°F. Set bowl of chilled batter over the ice bath. Working in batches, dip vegetables in the batter, then fry until golden, crisp, and cooked through, 2½ to 3½ minutes. Transfer to paper towels to drain, and sprinkle with salt. Serve hot with dipping sauce.

TEMPURA DIPPING SAUCE

MAKES ½ CUP

1 one-ounce piece fresh ginger

2 tablespoons soy sauce

1 tablespoon Asian fish sauce

2 tablespoons mirin (Japanese cooking wine)

1 tablespoon thinly sliced scallion

1 teaspoon freshly squeezed lemon juice

2 tablespoons rice-wine vinegar

3 tablespoons water

1. Using the fine holes of a box grater, grate ginger. Wrap ginger in cheesecloth. Working over a medium bowl, tightly squeeze ginger to extract juice. Discard cheesecloth and remaining ginger.

2. Add soy sauce, fish sauce, mirin, scallion, lemon juice, vinegar, and the water to the ginger juice. Whisk to combine. Dipping sauce can be refrigerated in an airtight container up to 1 week.

ROASTED RED PEPPER DIP

MAKES 1½ CUPS

3 red bell peppers

1 small garlic clove

1 teaspoon freshly squeezed lemon juice

⅛ teaspoon ground cumin

¼ teaspoon crushed red-pepper flakes

½ teaspoon coarse salt

¼ teaspoon freshly ground black pepper

1. Roast peppers on a grill or on top of a gas burner until skin is blackened, turning as each side becomes charred. Place in a medium bowl; cover with plastic wrap until cool enough to handle. Using a paper towel, rub off and discard charred skins. Slice peppers into 2-inch pieces; discard seeds and ribs.

2. Place peppers in a food processor along with garlic, lemon juice, cumin, red-pepper flakes, salt, and pepper; process until puréed, 1 to 2 minutes.

SPICED NUTS
MAKES 2 1/2 CUPS

1 large egg white
1/4 cup sugar
1 teaspoon coarse salt
1/2 teaspoon chili powder
1/4 teaspoon ground allspice
1/2 teaspoon ground cumin
1 1/4 teaspoons cayenne pepper
2 1/2 cups assorted nuts, such as pecan halves,
cashews, walnuts, or almonds

1. Preheat oven to 300°F. In a medium bowl, whisk egg white until foamy (no clear liquid should remain on the bottom of the bowl). In a separate bowl, combine sugar, salt, and spices; whisk into egg white.
2. Stir in nuts until well coated; spread mixture in a single layer onto a rimmed baking sheet.
3. Bake nuts 15 minutes; remove from oven. Using a metal spatula, stir to separate nuts. Reduce oven to 250°F; return nuts to oven until medium brown, about 10 minutes.
4. Transfer baking sheet to a wire rack; toss, and stir again. Let cool; break up any nuts that stick together. Store in an airtight container at room temperature up to 2 weeks.

GRILLED CHEDDAR
AND TOMATO QUESADILLAS
MAKES 4

8 eight-inch flour tortillas
2 cups grated white cheddar cheese
2 tomatoes, thinly sliced
Guacamole (recipe follows)

Preheat grill or skillet to high heat. Sprinkle each of 4 tortillas with 1/4 cup cheese. Cover with tomato slices; sprinkle with another 1/4 cup cheese. Top with 4 remaining tortillas. Grill until bottom tortilla is brown and cheese is melted. Flip over, and cook until brown, cheese is melted, and tomato is hot. Transfer to a cutting surface; cut into wedges. Serve with guacamole.

GUACAMOLE
MAKES ABOUT 2 CUPS

2 ripe avocados
1/2 garlic clove, minced
1 jalapeño pepper, minced
2 tablespoons freshly squeezed lime juice
1 teaspoon coarse salt
1/2 teaspoon freshly ground black pepper
1/2 cup loosely packed fresh cilantro,
chopped

Pit and peel avocados. Combine avocado, garlic, jalapeño, lime juice, salt, and pepper in a large bowl. Mash with a large spoon until combined but still chunky. Stir in cilantro, and serve.

CHICKPEA-PIMIENTO CROSTINI
SERVES 10 TO 12

1 large garlic clove
1 can (15 1/2 ounces) chickpeas, drained
and rinsed
3 tablespoons pimientos, finely chopped,
plus more sliced for garnish
1/4 cup extra-virgin olive oil
1/4 teaspoon ground cumin
1 tablespoon finely chopped fresh flat-leaf
parsley, plus leaves for garnish
Coarse salt and freshly ground pepper
Crostini (recipe follows)

1. Process garlic in a food processor until finely chopped. Add chickpeas; pulse until crushed but not puréed, 7 to 8 times. Transfer to a small bowl. Add pimientos, olive oil, cumin, and parsley; season with salt and pepper. Stir to combine.
2. Spoon about 1 tablespoon mixture on top of each crostini. Garnish with a parsley leaf and a slice of pimiento, and serve.

CROSTINI
MAKES 30 TO 35

Crostini can be made up to two days in
advance and stored in an airtight container.

1 five- to six-ounce baguette, sliced
on the diagonal, 1/4 inch thick
2 tablespoons olive oil

Preheat oven to 350°F. Brush each bread slice lightly on both sides with olive oil. Place on a large baking sheet; toast until lightly golden, 5 to 6 minutes on each side, turning once. Remove from oven; transfer to a wire rack to cool.

DEVILED EGGS
MAKES 1 DOZEN EGGS (2 DOZEN HALVES)

12 hard-boiled eggs, peeled
Coarse salt and freshly ground pepper

FOR CURRIED DEVILED EGGS:

3 1/2 tablespoons mayonnaise
1 teaspoon curry powder

FOR BASIL DEVILED EGGS:

1/2 cup fresh basil leaves, roughly chopped
3 tablespoons mayonnaise

FOR CREME FRAICHE DEVILED EGGS:

3 tablespoons crème fraîche
2 teaspoons Dijon mustard
4 cornichons, minced (about 1 tablespoon)

1. Halve eggs lengthwise. Carefully remove yolks; set whites aside. Place 4 yolks in each of three bowls, and mash yolks with a fork.
2. Stir mayonnaise and curry powder into one bowl. Season with salt and pepper.
3. Place basil and mayonnaise in a food processor; blend about 2 minutes. Stir mixture into second bowl of yolks. Season with salt and pepper.
4. Stir crème fraîche, mustard, and cornichons into last bowl. Season with salt and pepper.
5. Spoon fillings into reserved egg-white halves.

OLIVE TAPENADE AND
GOAT CHEESE CROSTINI
SERVES 10 TO 12

To make your own tapenade, chop pitted olives;
add salt and olive oil to bind the mixture.

3/4 cup store-bought green- or
black-olive tapenade
3 tablespoons fresh thyme leaves,
plus sprig tips for garnish
5 tablespoons (1 1/4 ounces) finely
chopped walnuts
1/4 cup dried currants
5 ounces fresh goat cheese
Crostini (recipe above)

In a small bowl, combine tapenade, thyme leaves, walnuts, and currants. Spread 1 to 2 teaspoons goat cheese onto each crostini. Spoon 1 to 2 teaspoons olive mixture on top, and garnish each with thyme tips. Serve.

TUNA NICOISE CROSTINI
SERVES 10 TO 12

¼ cup green olives, pitted

4 hard-boiled eggs, peeled

5 tablespoons mayonnaise

1 three-ounce can solid white tuna in oil, drained and broken into small pieces

2 tablespoons non pareil capers, drained and chopped

1 tablespoon chopped fresh tarragon leaves, plus more for garnish
  Coarse salt and freshly ground pepper
  Crostini (page 133)

1. Finely chop half the olives; thinly slice the rest. Set aside.
2. Remove yolks from eggs, and set aside. Place whites in a bowl. Using a fork, mash egg whites until ¼-inch pieces are formed. Add mayonnaise, tuna, reserved chopped olives, capers, and chopped tarragon; stir to combine. Season with salt and pepper. Spoon 1 tablespoon tuna mixture onto each crostini.
3. With a spoon, press reserved yolks through a sieve into a bowl. Top each crostini with some yolk, garnish with tarragon leaves and reserved sliced olives, and serve.

WILD-MUSHROOM BRUSCHETTA
SERVES 8 TO 10; MAKES 20

When using different types of mushrooms, it is best to cook each one separately, as their cooking times may vary. We used three varieties in this recipe, each portion weighing a third of a pound. If you are using only one or two types, increase the amount of the other ingredients for each batch accordingly.

1 pound assorted fresh wild mushrooms, such as chanterelle, porcini, and oyster

6 tablespoons unsalted butter

4 garlic cloves
  Coarse salt and freshly ground pepper

1 cup dry white wine

1 loaf rustic bread cut into thin slices

3 tablespoons olive oil

1. Heat a grill or grill pan or preheat oven to 350°F. Brush mushrooms free of grit; cut into 1-inch pieces. Melt 2 tablespoons butter in a medium sauté pan over medium heat. Mince 1 garlic clove, and add one-third to pan. Add one type of mushroom, and season with salt and pepper.

Cook, shaking pan, until mushrooms are golden and releasing their juice. The mushrooms should be tender but not mushy.
2. Add ⅓ cup wine to pan; deglaze pan, scraping up any brown bits from the bottom with a wooden spoon. Transfer mushrooms to a large serving bowl; season with salt and pepper, as desired. Repeat process with remaining two types of mushrooms and butter, garlic, and wine, seasoning each batch with salt and pepper.
3. Toast bread until golden on both sides. Transfer to a serving tray. Lightly brush one side of each with oil. To serve, place mushrooms and remaining garlic cloves on tray alongside bread.

DESSERTS

COFFEE ICE CREAM AFFOGATO
SERVES 4

1 pint best-quality coffee ice cream or gelato

4 ounces liqueur, such as sambuca, amaretto, or Frangelico (optional)

4 demitasse cups freshly brewed espresso

Just before serving, scoop ice cream into four small bowls or large coffee cups. Divide liqueur among four small glasses, if using; serve liqueur and espresso alongside each bowl, and let each person pour them over the ice cream.

PEPPERMINT HOT-FUDGE SUNDAES
SERVES 4

1 cup heavy cream

⅓ cup light corn syrup, plus more as needed

1 twelve-ounce bag semisweet chocolate chips

1 teaspoon peppermint extract
  Best-quality vanilla ice cream
  Peppermint candy, coarsely chopped

1. Combine heavy cream and corn syrup in a small saucepan. Stir to combine, and bring just to a boil over medium-high heat. Remove from heat, and add chocolate and peppermint extract.
2. Whisk until the chocolate is melted. If necessary, adjust consistency with additional corn syrup. Scoop ice cream into parfait glasses; serve chocolate sauce over ice cream, and garnish with chopped peppermint candy.

SUNKEN CHOCOLATE CAKES WITH COFFEE ICE CREAM
SERVES 4

½ cup (1 stick) unsalted butter, cut in pieces, plus more for pans

¼ cup sugar, plus more for pans

5 ounces best-quality bittersweet chocolate, coarsely chopped

2 large whole eggs, separated

2 large egg yolks
  Coffee ice cream

1. Preheat oven to 350°F. Lightly butter 4 cups in a jumbo nonstick muffin pan, leaving the 2 center cups empty. Coat lightly with sugar; set aside.
2. Place butter and chocolate in a heat-proof bowl set over a pan of simmering water; stir occasionally, until melted and thoroughly combined. Remove from heat; set aside.
3. Combine 4 egg yolks with 2 tablespoons sugar; whisk until mixture is pale yellow and thick. Stir in the melted chocolate mixture.
4. In a mixing bowl, whisk egg whites until soft peaks form; add remaining 2 tablespoons sugar, and whisk until stiff and shiny but not dry. Fold into chocolate mixture. Divide batter among prepared muffin cups, and bake until just set and slightly springy to the touch, about 25 minutes.
5. Remove from oven, and transfer to a wire rack. Let cool 15 minutes in pan; carefully run a knife around edges of cakes, and invert onto a plate to remove from pan. Reinvert, and serve each with a scoop of ice cream.

SKILLET-BAKED CHOCOLATE-CHIP COOKIE
SERVES 8

2 cups all-purpose flour

1 teaspoon baking soda

½ teaspoon salt

¾ cup (1½ sticks) unsalted butter, softened

½ cup granulated sugar

¾ cup packed light-brown sugar

1 large egg

2 teaspoons pure vanilla extract

1½ cups mixed milk- and semisweet-chocolate chips (about 9 ounces)

2 pints vanilla ice cream
  Caramel Sauce (recipe follows)

1. Preheat oven to 350°F. In a medium bowl, whisk together flour, baking soda, and salt; set aside. In the bowl of an electric mixer fitted with

the paddle attachment, cream butter and sugars until mixture is light and fluffy, about 2 minutes. Add egg and vanilla; mix until they are fully incorporated. Add flour mixture, and beat until just combined. Stir in chocolate chips.

2. Transfer dough to a 10-inch ovenproof skillet, and press to flatten, covering bottom of pan. Bake until edges are brown and top is golden, 40 to 45 minutes. Don't overbake; it will continue to cook a few minutes out of the oven. Transfer to a wire rack to cool, 15 to 20 minutes. Cut into 8 wedges. Serve warm; top each wedge with a scoop of ice cream and some caramel sauce.

CARAMEL SAUCE
MAKES ABOUT 1 CUP

1 cup sugar
¼ teaspoon salt
¼ cup water
½ cup heavy cream
2 tablespoons unsalted butter
½ teaspoon pure vanilla extract

In a small saucepan, combine sugar, salt, and the water. Cook over medium heat (do not stir) until sugar is a medium amber color, about 7 minutes; wash sides of pan with a pastry brush dipped in water to prevent crystals from forming. Remove from heat. Carefully stir in heavy cream; add butter, and stir until combined. Let cool to room temperature; stir in vanilla. Sauce can be stored in an airtight container in refrigerator up to 2 weeks. Reheat gently; serve warm or at room temperature.

ESPRESSO BISCUITS
MAKES 16

1½ cups all-purpose flour
½ cup Dutch-process cocoa powder
1 tablespoon finely ground espresso beans
1 cup (2 sticks) unsalted butter,
    room temperature
¾ cup confectioners' sugar
1 teaspoon pure vanilla extract

1. Preheat oven to 350°F, with racks in upper and lower thirds. Line two baking sheets with parchment paper, and set aside. In a medium bowl, sift together flour, cocoa powder, and ground espresso beans; set aside.

2. In the bowl of an electric mixer fitted with the paddle attachment, combine butter, sugar, and vanilla until creamy, 3 to 4 minutes. Gradually

beat flour mixture into butter mixture, scraping down sides of bowl twice.

3. Roll about 2½ tablespoons of dough between your palms to form a ball. Place on a prepared baking sheet; repeat with remaining batter, spacing cookies 2 inches apart. Using a fork, gently press tines onto dough to form a biscuit shape. Bake just until firm to the touch, 12 to 15 minutes. Transfer to a wire rack to cool.

RASPBERRY ANGEL FOOD CAKE
MAKES 1 TEN-INCH CAKE

1 cup sifted cake flour (not self-rising)
1½ cups sugar, preferably superfine
    Pinch of salt
½ pint (6 ounces) fresh raspberries
12 large egg whites (about 1¼ cups)
1 teaspoon cream of tartar
1½ teaspoons pure vanilla extract
    Confectioners' sugar, for dusting

1. Preheat oven to 350°F, with rack in lower third. Into a large bowl, sift flour, ½ cup sugar, and salt twice; set aside. In a small bowl, mash ½ cup berries; pass through a fine sieve to yield ¼ cup purée. Discard solids; set aside.

2. In the bowl of an electric mixer fitted with the whisk attachment, beat egg whites on medium-low speed until foamy. Beat in cream of tartar and vanilla. Raise the speed to medium-high, and beat to soft peaks. Reduce speed to medium-low; beat in remaining cup sugar, 2 tablespoons at a time. Beat until peaks are stiff. Transfer to a large, shallow bowl.

3. Sift flour mixture again over whites; fold in just until combined. Transfer one-third of batter to an ungreased 10-inch tube pan (with legs, if possible); spoon 2 tablespoons reserved berry purée over the top in the middle of the batter. Spoon another third of batter into pan; top with remaining purée and then remaining batter. Run a knife through batter to eliminate air pockets; do not smooth peaks.

4. Bake until cake is lightly golden and springy to the touch, 35 to 45 minutes. (If top gets too dark, tent with foil.) Remove from oven. Invert pan onto its legs or hang it over the neck of a bottle; let cool completely, about 1 hour. Run a knife around edges to loosen; unmold onto platter. Dust with confectioners' sugar, and serve with remaining whole berries.

CHEWY ORANGE-ALMOND COOKIES
MAKES 2 DOZEN

1¼ cups sliced almonds (about 4¼ ounces)
¾ cup granulated sugar
¼ cup all-purpose flour
    Finely grated zest of 2 oranges,
    (about 4 tablespoons)
1 teaspoon anise seeds, crushed
3 large egg whites, room temperature
¼ teaspoon salt
2 tablespoons confectioners' sugar

1. Preheat oven to 350°F. Line two baking sheets with parchment paper, and set aside.

2. In a food processor, combine 1 cup almonds with ½ cup granulated sugar; process until almonds are finely ground. Transfer mixture to a medium bowl. Stir in flour, orange zest, and crushed anise seeds.

3. In the bowl of an electric mixer fitted with the whisk attachment, beat egg whites, salt, and remaining ¼ cup sugar to soft glossy peaks. Fold egg-white mixture into dry ingredients.

4. Spoon level tablespoons of batter, 2 inches apart, on prepared baking sheets. Arrange 3 almonds on each cookie. Sift confectioners' sugar over cookies. Bake until lightly browned around edges, about 12 minutes, rotating sheets halfway through. Remove from oven; let cool slightly before removing from sheets. The cookies can be frozen, wrapped well in plastic, up to 2 months.

BANANA PILLOWS
SERVES 4

When making these "pillows," cut dough along the folds to prevent uneven rising.

1 sheet frozen puff pastry, from standard
    package (17¼ ounces), thawed
½ cup (1 stick) unsalted butter
⅓ cup firmly packed light-brown sugar
¼ teaspoon pure vanilla extract
    Pinch of salt
3 tablespoons heavy cream
4 ripe but firm bananas (1½ pounds),
    sliced ¼ inch thick on diagonal
    Confectioners' sugar
    Chocolate shavings, for garnish

1. Preheat oven to 400°F. Roll out pastry ⅛ inch thick; cut out four 5-inch squares. Place on a parchment-lined baking sheet; bake until golden, about 15 minutes. Remove from oven; let cool.

2. Place butter, brown sugar, vanilla, and salt in a sauté pan over medium heat. Cook, stirring frequently, until butter and sugar are melted and combined, about 5 minutes. Stir in cream until mixture is smooth. Add bananas; gently stir until coated. Remove from heat.

3. Using a paring knife, remove and discard a 2-inch square from top center of reserved pillows; keep bottom intact. Fill with banana mixture. Dust with confectioners' sugar, and garnish with chocolate shavings. Serve immediately.

COCONUT-MACAROON TARTLETS
MAKES 12

1½ cups shredded unsweetened coconut
2 large egg whites
¼ cup sugar
1 cup heavy cream
1 vanilla bean, split in half lengthwise
½ ounce crystallized ginger, finely chopped
Vegetable-oil cooking spray

1. Preheat oven to 350°F. In a large bowl, stir together coconut, egg whites, and sugar. Stir until mixture holds together when squeezed.

2. Coat twelve 2-inch brioche or tartlet tins with cooking spray. Form 1 heaping tablespoon coconut mixture into a ball; press into a prepared tin, making a thumbprint in the center and pressing out so mixture forms a ¼-inch-thick "crust." Repeat with remaining coconut mixture and tins. Place tins on an unlined baking sheet.

3. Bake until golden brown, about 25 minutes. Remove from oven; let cool slightly. Turn crusts out onto a wire rack, and let cool completely.

4. Pour cream into a chilled mixing bowl. Scrape vanilla seeds into cream. Whisk until soft peaks form. Fill each crust with whipped cream; garnish with crystallized ginger. Serve.

MARSALA CHEESE TART WITH ORANGES
MAKES 1 EIGHT-INCH TART

5 ounces gingersnaps, broken into pieces
4 tablespoons unsalted butter, melted
8 ounces cream cheese, room temperature
½ cup sugar
2 tablespoons Marsala wine
1 teaspoon pure vanilla extract
½ cup heavy cream
3 navel oranges

1. Process gingersnaps in a food processor until finely ground. Transfer to a bowl; add melted butter, and stir until well combined. Transfer to an 8-inch fluted tart pan with a removable bottom; press into bottom and up sides to form an even crust. Place in freezer.

2. In the bowl of an electric mixer fitted with the paddle attachment, beat cream cheese and sugar until fluffy. Add Marsala and vanilla; beat until combined. In another bowl, whip heavy cream to stiff peaks, and fold into cream-cheese mixture. Spoon into prepared crust; return to freezer until firm, at least 1 hour 15 minutes.

3. Cut ends off oranges, and remove peel, pith, and outer membranes with a paring knife, following the curve of the fruit. Carefully pull sections away from the inner membranes, keeping sections whole. Serve cheesecake garnished with orange sections.

MELON SALAD WITH ORANGE-GINGER SYRUP
SERVES 8

1 cup freshly squeezed orange juice (about 4 oranges)
Zest of 2 oranges, finely grated
1 cup sugar
½ ounce fresh ginger, thinly sliced
2 tablespoons Cointreau
1 small honeydew melon, cut in half and seeded
1 small canary melon, cut in half and seeded
1 cantaloupe, peeled, seeded, and cut into 1-inch wedges
Mint sprigs, for garnish
Orange Lace Cookies (recipe follows)

1. Prepare a large ice bath; set aside. Bring orange juice, sugar, and ginger to a boil in a small saucepan over medium heat. Let simmer, stirring occasionally, until sugar has dissolved and syrup has thickened, about 15 minutes. Remove from heat; strain syrup into a clean bowl. Add the Cointreau; stir to combine. Set bowl in ice bath until syrup is cold, stirring frequently.

2. Using different sizes of melon ballers, scoop honeydew and canary melons into balls. Place in a medium bowl; add ½ cup cold syrup and orange zest. Toss to combine.

3. To serve, arrange cantaloupe on a platter. Spoon some melon balls on top; serve remaining balls on the side. Drizzle melons with some syrup; garnish with mint. Serve with cookies and remaining syrup on the side.

ORANGE LACE COOKIES
MAKES ABOUT 3 DOZEN

¼ cup light corn syrup
¼ cup packed light-brown sugar
4 tablespoons unsalted butter
1 tablespoon Cointreau
½ cup plus 2 tablespoons all-purpose flour
1 tablespoon finely chopped orange zest, (about 1 orange)
⅛ teaspoon salt

1. Preheat oven to 350°F. Line a baking sheet with a Silpat baking mat or parchment paper; set aside. Combine corn syrup, sugar, butter, and Cointreau in a small saucepan over low heat; stir until butter melts. Remove from heat. Stir in flour, orange zest, and salt until combined.

2. Drop heaping teaspoons of batter onto prepared baking sheet, about 2½ inches apart. Bake until cookies spread out and turn golden brown, about 14 minutes. Remove from oven; let stand until slightly firm, about 4 minutes. Transfer cookies to a wire rack, and let cool until crisp. Repeat until all batter has been used, stirring batter between batches. Cookies can be stored in an airtight container up to 2 days.

TIPS &
TECHNIQUES

PATE BRISEE
MAKES ENOUGH FOR 2 EIGHT- TO TEN-INCH
CRUSTS OR 6 FOUR-INCH TARTLETS

Make sure all your ingredients are thoroughly chilled before you begin.

2 ½ cups all-purpose flour,
*   plus more for work surface*
* 1 teaspoon salt*
* 1 teaspoon sugar*
* 1 cup (2 sticks) chilled unsalted butter,*
*   cut into pieces*
* 4 to 6 tablespoons ice water*

1. Place flour, salt, and sugar in a food processor, and pulse a few times to combine. Add butter, and process until mixture resembles coarse meal, about 10 seconds. With machine running, add ice water in a slow, steady stream through the feed tube just until dough holds together. Do not process more than 30 seconds.
2. Turn out dough onto a lightly floured work surface. Divide in half; place each half on plastic wrap. Flatten into disks. Wrap; refrigerate at least 1 hour before using or freeze up to 1 month.

FRUIT CRISP TOPPING
MAKES 2 QUARTS

Sprinkle this topping over a baking dish filled with berries, chopped peaches, pears, or apples, tossed with a bit of lemon juice and sugar. Bake in a 375°F oven until juices are bubbling and topping is golden brown, 30 to 45 minutes, depending on fruit. If topping starts to get too brown, tent dish with foil.

* ½ cup (about 2 ounces) whole almonds*
2 ¼ cups all-purpose flour
* ¼ cup packed light-brown sugar*
* ⅓ cup granulated sugar*
* ½ teaspoon ground cinnamon*
* ½ teaspoon coarse salt*
* 1 cup (2 sticks) chilled unsalted butter,*
*   cut into small pieces*

1. Preheat oven to 350°F. Spread nuts in a single layer on a rimmed baking sheet; toast until aromatic, about 8 minutes, shaking pan halfway through. Remove from oven; let cool.

2. Place almonds in a food processor; process until coarsely ground. Transfer to the bowl of an electric mixer fitted with the paddle attachment. Add flour, sugars, cinnamon, and salt; mix until just combined. Add butter; mix on low speed until pea-size clumps form, 4 to 5 minutes. Sprinkle over fruit, and bake, or freeze topping in an airtight plastic bag or container up to 2 months.

CHOCOLATE CHUNK COOKIES
MAKES ABOUT 4 DOZEN

2 ½ cups all-purpose flour
* 1 teaspoon baking soda*
* ½ teaspoon baking powder*
* 1 teaspoon salt*
* 1 cup (2 sticks) unsalted butter,*
*   room temperature*
* ⅔ cup granulated sugar*
* ⅔ cup packed light-brown sugar*
* 2 large eggs*
* 1 teaspoon pure vanilla extract*
* 8 ounces bittersweet chocolate,*
*   chopped into small chunks*

1. In a bowl, combine flour, baking soda, baking powder, and salt; set aside.
2. In the bowl of an electric mixer fitted with the paddle attachment, cream butter and sugars until smooth. Add eggs and vanilla; beat until fluffy. Add flour mixture; beat until combined. Stir in the chocolate.
3. Divide dough in half; place each half on plastic wrap or parchment paper. Roll each half into a log about 1½ inches in diameter. Wrap in plastic; refrigerate until firm, at least 2 hours or overnight, or freeze up to 3 months.
4. Preheat oven to 350°F. Line baking sheets with a Silpat baking mat or parchment paper; set aside. Unwrap logs; slice into ¼-inch-thick rounds. Place on a prepared baking sheet, about 1½ inches apart. Bake until golden, 10 to 12 minutes. Transfer to a wire rack to cool. Serve, or store in an airtight container up to 2 weeks.

CHOCOLATE FUDGE SAUCE
MAKES ABOUT 4 CUPS

* 1 pound bittersweet chocolate*
2 ½ cups heavy cream

1. Using a serrated knife, chop chocolate finely, and place in a heat-proof bowl.
2. In a small saucepan, bring cream to a boil over medium-high heat; pour over chopped chocolate. Let stand 10 minutes. Use a rubber spatula to stir chocolate and cream until smooth and combined. Store in an airtight container, refrigerated, up to 1 week. Warm gently in a heat-proof bowl set over a pan of simmering water before using.

CARAMEL AND BOURBON
VANILLA SAUCE
MAKES 2 CUPS

* 2 cups sugar*
* ½ cup water*
* 1 cup heavy cream*
* 1 vanilla bean, split in half lengthwise*
*   and scraped*
* 2 teaspoons freshly squeezed lemon juice*
* 2 tablespoons unsalted butter*
* 1 tablespoon bourbon*

Combine sugar and the water in a 2-quart saucepan over medium heat, stirring to dissolve sugar. Without stirring, cook until dark amber in color, swirling pan gently to color evenly, about 20 minutes. Reduce heat to low. Slowly add cream, stirring with a wooden spoon. Add vanilla bean and seeds, lemon juice, butter, and bourbon; stir to combine. Store in an airtight container, refrigerated, up to 1 week. Before using, bring caramel sauce to room temperature, or warm over low heat, and discard vanilla pod.

RASPBERRY SAUCE
MAKES 1¼ CUPS

* 2 cups fresh raspberries*
* ¼ cup sugar*
* 2 tablespoons water*
* 1 tablespoon freshly squeezed lemon juice*

Combine all ingredients in a small saucepan over medium-low heat. Cook until berries release their juice but are still whole, about 5 minutes. Serve warm or at room temperature.

THE TEMPLATES

To use our templates, enlarge these images on a photocopier to desired size (unless otherwise specified), then follow the project's directions. Trace templates onto appropriate paper, then cut along solid lines and fold along dotted lines. To make a STAR-POINT LANTERN, you will need to trace the template twice. To make a PAPER ROSE, cut out spiral, beginning with outermost line, at point B for a small rose and point A for a large rose (do not cut marking for point B).

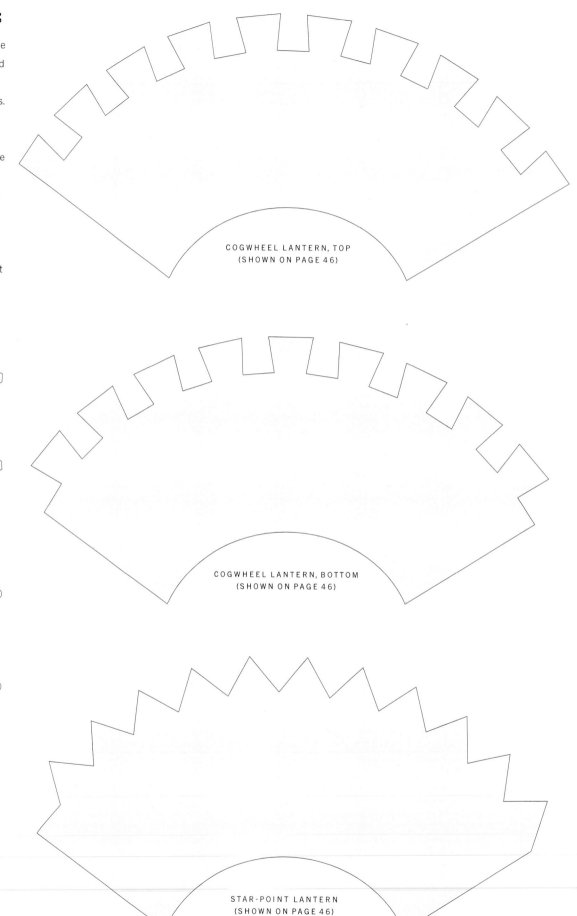

COGWHEEL LANTERN, TOP
(SHOWN ON PAGE 46)

COGWHEEL LANTERN, BOTTOM
(SHOWN ON PAGE 46)

SNOWFLAKE FRILLS
(SHOWN ON PAGE 82)

STAR-POINT LANTERN
(SHOWN ON PAGE 46)

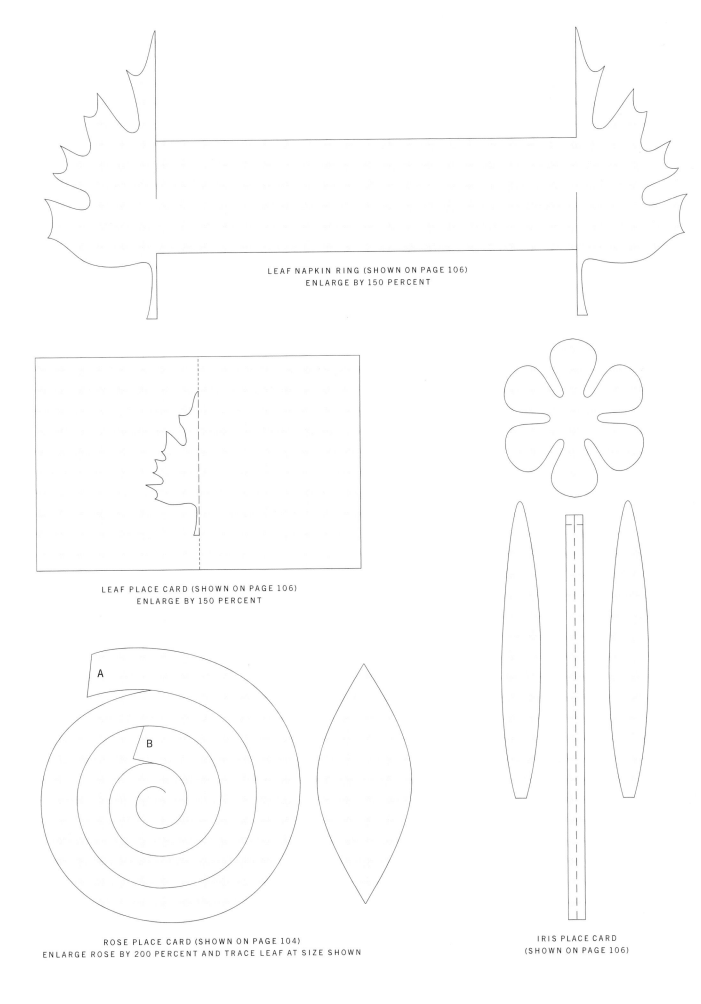

LEAF NAPKIN RING (SHOWN ON PAGE 106)
ENLARGE BY 150 PERCENT

LEAF PLACE CARD (SHOWN ON PAGE 106)
ENLARGE BY 150 PERCENT

A

B

ROSE PLACE CARD (SHOWN ON PAGE 104)
ENLARGE ROSE BY 200 PERCENT AND TRACE LEAF AT SIZE SHOWN

IRIS PLACE CARD
(SHOWN ON PAGE 106)

The Guide

DRINKS

16 ORIGAMI PAPERS, from Kinokuniya Bookstores, 10 West 49th Street, New York, NY 10020, 212-765-7766. BAMBOO SKEWERS (#106150), from Broadway Panhandler, 866-266-5927. Giant MAPLE LEAF PUNCH (#91400) and giant BIRCH LEAF PUNCH (#91004), from McGill, 800-982-9884 or www.mcgillinc.com.

HORS D'OUEVRES

22 Three-part DISH (#548944), from Crate and Barrel, 800-967-6696 or www.crateandbarrel .com. 3/4" sage-green "Pride" SATIN RIBBON, from Masterstroke Canada, 866-249-7677 or www.masterstrokecanada.com.

LIGHTING

32 SEASHELLS, from Sanibel Seashell Industries, 905 Fitzhugh Street, Sanibel Island, FL 33957, 239-472-1603 or www.seashells.com.

32–33 Pink BAGS (#12 and #2), from Wisconsin Converting, available from Aim Variety, 920-468-4600. Kraft PAPER BAGS, large (SOS25) and small (SOS1), from U.S. Box, 800-221-0999 or www.usbox.com. White WINE BAG (#6609), from American Stationery Company, 800-822-2577 or www.americanstationery.com. RAYON CORD (#60), in colors 45, 59, and 2, from Mokuba New York, 212-869-8900. Wedgwood Queen's Ware DINNER PLATE (KWE001), from Martha Stewart: The Catalog for Living, 800-950-7130 or www.marthastewart.com.

34 Clear GLASS CYLINDERS: 5"-by-5"; 6"-by-6"; 6"-by-10"; and 4"-by-8"; all from Planter Resource, 212-206-7687 or www .potteryking.com. OAK LEAVES, from Dry Nature Designs, 129 West 28th Street, New York, NY 10001, 212-695-8911. Riedel "Bordeaux" vinum GLASSES (DTS015), from Martha Stewart: The Catalog for Living, 800-950-7130 or www.marthastewart.com.

35 Pressed SKELETONIZED LEAVES, from Nature's Pressed, P.O. Box 212, Orem, UT 84059, 800-850-2499 or www.naturespressed .com. 12" HURRICANES, from B & J Florist Supply, 103 West 28th Street, New York, NY 10001, 212-564-6086. TRACING VELLUM, from NY Central Art Supply, 62 Third Avenue, New York, NY 10003, 212-473-7705 or 800-950-6111. SCISSORS, by Fiskars, 7811 West Stewert Avenue, Wausau, WI 54401, 715-849-4011 for retailers or www.fiskars.com. PLACE SETTING, from Party Rental Ltd., 888-774-4776. Oak SKELETON LEAVES, in natural, from Dry Nature Designs; see above.

36 28"-by-40" German TISSUE PAPER, and Mokuba PAPER, from Kate's Paperie, 561 Broadway, New York, NY 10012, 888-941-9169 or www.katespaperie.com. WAXED-LINEN TWINE, from the Caning Shop, 926 Gilman Street, Berkeley, CA 94710, 510-527-5010.

37 28"-by-40" German WAXED TISSUE PAPER, from Kate's Paperie; see above. WROUGHT-IRON DISH for salt, from Terra Verde, 120 Wooster Street, New York, NY 10012, 212-925-4533.

38 MIRROR FRAME, from City Frames, 259 West 30th Street, New York, NY 10001, 212-967-4401. 10" POTS, from Planter Resource; see above. Repti SAND, from Petco, 800-571-2952 or www.petco.com for stores. TABLE LINENS, GLASSWARE, FLATWARE, CHINA, and CHAIRS, from Party Rental Ltd.; see above.

39 Glass star BOWL (F0435), from Simon Pearce, 120 Wooster Street, New York, NY 10010, 212-334-2393 or www.simonpearce.com. FLOATING CANDLES, from Pier 1 Imports, 800-447-4371 for locations.

42 BEESWAX (natural or filtered), from Alberta Beeswax & Candle Making Supplies, 10611–170 Street, Edmonton, Alberta T5P 4W2, 780-413-0350 or www.candlesandbeeswax.com. Natural or bleached BEESWAX, from Pearl Paint, 800-221-6845; NY Central Art Supply, see above; and the Compleat Sculptor, 90 Vandam Street, New York, NY 10013, 212-243-6074 or www.sculpt.com. CANDLE DYE and square braid WICKING, from Alberta Beeswax & Candle Making Supplies, see above; and Pearl Paint, see above.

43 Bistro CHAIRS, from Third Street Bazaar, 125 West Third Street, New York, NY 10012, 212-673-4138. SOUP BOWLS, blue enamel PLATES, and NAPKINS, from Crate and Barrel, 800-967-6696 or www.crateandbarrel.com.

44 LANDSCAPE LIGHTING DESIGN, available from Greg Yale Landscape Illumination, 27 Henry Road, Southampton, NY 11968, 631-287-2132.

46–47 HOLE PUNCH, from Sax Arts & Crafts Catalog, 800-558-6696. 6" bone folder, from NY Central Art Supply; see above. 48" pressure-sensitive peel-and-stick STYRENE, from the Lamp Shop, P.O. Box 3606, Concord, NH 03302, 603-224-1603 or www.lampshop.com.

48 Paper LAMPSHADES, from Just Shades, 21 Spring Street, New York, NY 10012, 212-966-2757. Sekishu-Hanshi Mare PAPER (on wire columns), from NY Central Art Supply paper department, 212-473-7705 or 800-950-6111.

FLOWERS & CENTERPIECES

52 Assorted LINENS, SILVERWARE, and CRYSTAL, from Broadway Famous Party Rentals, 134 Morgan Avenue, Brooklyn, NY 11237, 718-821-4000.

53 Wooden BOWL, from Simon Pearce, 120 Wooster Street, New York, NY 10012, 212-334-2393. Cork FLORAL FLOATS (#704A12), from Dorothy Biddle Service Catalogue, 570-226-3239.

60 PASSIONFLOWERS, from Logee's Greenhouses, 141 North Street, Danielson, CT 06239, 888-330-8038. CLEMATIS, from Chalk Hill Clematis, P.O. Box 1847, Healdsburg, CA 95448, 707-433-8416 or www.chalkhillclematis.com.

61 Copper PAILS, available from Bayberry Nursery, 96 Montauk Highway, Amagansett, NY 11930, 631-267-3000. PLANTS, available from Atlock Flower Farm, 545 Weston Canal Road, Somerset, NJ 08873, 732-356-3373. 4"-by-8" and 12"-by-4" CYLINDERS, from Planter Resource, 212-206-7687 or www .potteryking.com.

63 Late-19th-century French hand-blown glass TUMBLERS, late-19th-century French DINNER PLATES marked Limoges, blown- and pressed-glass French JELLY JARS, French blown-glass wine CARAFE, and late-19th-century French hand-blown WINE TUMBLER, from Lucullus, 610 Chartres Street, New Orleans, LA 70115, 504-528-9620. Beige linen TORCHONS with red stripe, from Wirthmore Antiques, 3727 Magazine Street, New Orleans, LA 70115, 504-269-0660 or www.wirthmoreantiques.com. Panibois BAKING MOLDS (CKP013 to CKP019), from Martha Stewart: The Catalog for Living, 800-950-7130 or www.marthastewart.com.

64–65 Kimono and Folk-art design ORIGAMI PAPER by Aitoh; 20"-by-30" Evergreen embossed DIAMOND PAPER in "Robin's Egg Blue," 25"-by-37" Shadow Stripe blue PAPER, and 1/4" square BALSA STRIPS by Midwest (#2147) in 36" lengths, all from Pearl Paint, 800-221-6845. 20"-by-28" Xylem India BLOCK PRINT and 19"-by-27" Bertini PAPER (#176), from NY Central Art Supply, 800-950-6111 or www.nycentralart.com.

66 From left to right: BASKETS without handles (#532, #432); BASKET with handle (#530), from Texas Basket Company, 800-657-2200. BASSWOOD STRIPS and BASSWOOD SHEETS, from A.I. Friedman, 212-243-9000. Wedgwood QUEEN'S WARE (KWE001); French Ivory FLATWARE (KFW017), from Martha Stewart: The Catalog for Living, 800-950-7130 or www.marthastewart.com.

67 FISH PLATTER, from Dean & DeLuca, 800-999-0306.

69 Antique burnished gold damask TABLECLOTH, (set includes 10 napkins), from Trouvaille Française, 552 East 87th Street, New York, NY 10128, 212-737-6015. By appointment only. 10" and 8" vintage silver-plated pedestal CAKE STANDS and 6" silver-plated COMPOTE, from Hôtel, available from Bergdorf Goodman, 212-753-7300.

TABLE COVERINGS

76–78 Special thanks to Eberhard Müller and Paulette Satur of Satur Farms, 3075 Alvah's Lane, Cutchogue, NY 11935, 631-734-4219 or www.saturfarms.com.

78 WOOL CASHMERE FELT, from B & J Fabrics, 263 West 40th Street, New York, NY 10018, 212-354-8150. Three-ply COTTON, from Steinlauf & Stoller, 239 West 39th Street, New York, NY 10018, 877-869-0321. 6" PILLAR CANDLES, from the Candle Shop, 118 Christopher Street, New York, NY 10014, 212-989-0148.

79 Glycerin-preserved OAK LEAVES, available from Oks Flowers, 123 West 28th Street, New York, NY 10001, 212-268-7231. Martha Stewart Everyday Colors PAINT in "Cornmeal" (E11), available at Kmart, 800-866-0086 or www.kmart.com for store locations. 8" double-faced SATIN RIBBON, from Hyman Hendler & Sons, 67 West 38th Street, New York, NY 10018, 212-840-8393.

83 Circa-1920 Art Deco Venetian MIRROR, from Maison Gerard, 53 East 10th Street,

New York, NY 10003, 212-674-7611. Assorted antique continental CHAMPAGNE FLUTES, from Evergreen Antiques, 1249 Third Avenue, New York, NY 10021, 212-744-5664. White SILK ORGANZA, from B & J Fabrics; see above. Pebeo APPLICATOR BOTTLES with fine tip, and Sulyn SILVER GLITTER, from Pearl Paint, 800-451-7327.

84 Tokizara DISH, from Kinokuniya Bookstores, 10 West 49th Street, New York, NY 10020, 212-765-7766. BAMBOO PLACE MATS (#02CC1205-ZK1178), from Pearl River, 800-878-2446 or www.pearlriver.com.

85 GLASS from Rosen-Paramount Glass Company, 45 East 20th Street, New York, NY 10003, 212-532-0820. PAINT in "Porcelain Green," "Araucana Turquoise," "Oceana," "Araucana Teal," and "Silkie White," from Fine Paints of Europe, 800-332-1556.

87 Enameled TERRINE MOLD, from Le Creuset of America, P.O. Box 575, Yemassee, SC 29945, 877-273-8738 or www.lecreuset.com. High-gloss, metal, and wood enamel PAINTS, by Benjamin Moore Paints, 888-236-6667. WOOD FINISH in "Colonial Maple," by Minwax, 800-462-0194 or www.minwax.com.

NAPKINS

90 Special thanks to Bob Flynn. Scented GERANIUMS, from Sandy Mush Herb Nursery, 316 Surrett Cove Road, Leicester, NC 28748, 828-683-2014.

91 Martha's favorite KITCHEN GLASSES (DJG002), from Martha Stewart: The Catalog for Living, 800-950-7130 or www.marthastewart.com.

92 3" star COOKIE CUTTER, from Sugarcraft; www.sugarcraft.com.

93 SUEDE CORD, from M & J Trimming, 1008 Sixth Avenue, New York, NY 10018, 212-391-9072. STAR ANISE, from International Grocery & Meat Market, 543 Ninth Avenue, New York, NY 10018, 212-279-5514. PAPER-COVERED WIRE, from Loose Ends, 2065 Madrona Avenue SE, Salem, OR 97302, 503-390-7457, 800-390-9979 or www.looseends.com. 2" pink SATIN RIBBON, from Hyman Hendler & Sons, 67 West 38th Street, New York, NY 10018, 212-840-8393.

94–95 Mother-of-pearl BUTTON, from Lou Lou Button, 69 West 38th Street, New York, NY 10018, 212-398-5498. Mini CLOTHESPIN, special order by the case, from Penley Corp., 207-674-2501. Gray-striped GROSGRAIN RIBBON,

from Hyman Hendler & Sons; see above. White 2" TASSEL, from M & J Trimming; see above.

96 Martha's favorite TUMBLERS (DTS040), from Martha Stewart: The Catalog for Living, 800-950-7130 or www.marthastewart.com. LINEN for napkins, from B & J Fabrics, 263 West 40th Street, New York, NY 10018, 212-354-8150.

98–99 Special thanks to Patricia Owens.

PLACE CARDS

105 Pink Luxury SATIN RIBBON, from Masterstroke Canada, 416-751-4193 or www.masterstrokecanada.com. Wedgwood QUEEN'S WARE (KWE001), from Martha Stewart: The Catalog for Living, 800-950-7130 or www.marthastewart.com.

106 Medium-weight PAPERS in pastel shades, from NY Central Art Supply, 62 Third Avenue, New York, NY 10003, 212-473-7705. Scalloped ROTARY CUTTER, from Sax Arts & Crafts Catalog, P.O. Box 510710, New Berlin, WI 53151, 414-784-6880 or 800-558-6696. Daisy monogrammed TEA TOWEL, from the Grand Acquisitor, 110 North Main Street, East Hampton, NY 11937, 631-324-7272.

DESSERTS

119 CANARY MELON, available in season, from Indian Rock Produce, 800-882-0512. Single MELON BALLER, 7/16" diameter (AGBC-12), and double MELON BALLER (AGBC-D22), from Bridge Kitchenware, 212-688-4220, 800-274-3435 or www.bridgekitchenware.com.

RECIPES

130–137 TURBINADO SUGAR and JALAPEÑO JELLY, from Whole Foods Market, 250 Seventh Avenue, New York, NY 10001, 212-924-5969 or www.wholefoods.com. CARDAMOM PODS (SPKA044R), from Adriana's Caravan, 800-316-0820 or www.adrianascaravan.com. MANCHEGO CHEESE, soft GOAT CHEESE, and NIÇOISE OLIVES, from Murray's Cheese Shop, 888-692-4339 or www.murrayscheese.com. GREEN-OLIVE and BLACK-OLIVE TAPENADE, from Dean & DeLuca, 800-999-0306. CURRANTS, from Melissa's World Variety Produce, 800-588-0151 or www.melissas.com. BITTERSWEET CHOCOLATE (#513466), from Sweet Celebrations, 800-328-6722 or www.sweetc.com. Premium-cut Australian CRYSTALLIZED GINGER, from Royal Pacific Foods, 800-551-5284 or www.gingerpeople.com for nearest retailer.

Executive Creative Director: Eric A. Pike

Editor: Ellen Morrissey

Text by Amy Nebens

Art Director: Mary Jane Callister

Associate Editor: Christine Moller

Senior Design Production Associate:
Duane Stapp

Design Production Associate:
Matthew Landfield

Thank you to all who generously lent their
time, talent, and energy to the creation of
this book, among them Annie Armstrong,
Nancy Arnot, Roger Astudillo, Evelyn
Battaglia, Brian Baytosh, Douglas Brenner,
Dora Braschi Cardinale, Caroline Cleary,
Peter Colen, Barbara De Wilde, James
Dunlinson, Julia Eisemann, Richard P.
Fontaine, Amanda Genge, Jamie Grill, Eric
Hutton, Jennifer J. Jarrett, Johanna Kletter,
Stacie McCormick, Jim McKeever, Elizabeth
Parson, Ayesha Patel, Meg Peterson, George
D. Planding, Eugenie Pliakis, Romy Pokorny,
Lesley Porcelli, Debra Puchalla, Meera Rao,
Margaret Roach, Colleen Shire, Susan
Spungen, Lauren Podlach Stanich, Susan
Sugarman, Gael Towey, Alison Vanek, and
Alicia White. Thanks also to Oxmoor House,
Clarkson Potter, Satellite Graphics, AGT.
seven, and R.R. Donnelley and Sons. Finally,
many thanks to Martha, whose ability to
entertain flawlessly, with every detail just
right, is truly inspiring.

PHOTOGRAPHERS

WILLIAM ABRANOWICZ
pages 2, 40-42, 44, 122 (top)

ANTHONY AMOS
page 106 (right)

SANG AN
pages 10 (left), 19, 20, 23, 24, 27 (right), 38
(right), 94, 95, 120, 128 (top), 129 (bottom)

STEFAN ANDERSON
pages 97, 122 (bottom)

QUENTIN BACON
page 102 (bottom), 103

JAMES BAIGRIE
page 110

CHRISTOPHER BAKER
pages 4, 5, 7 (center left, center right), 8, 30,
43, 50, 56 (left), 68, 70, 76, 77, 78 (top row),
100, 104 (left), 108

NINA BRAMHALL
page 22 (bottom)

LUIS BRUNO
pages 57 (left), 124 (bottom row left and middle)

MONICA BUCK
pages 112, 128 (bottom)

ANITA CALERO
page 113

EARL CARTER
pages 7 (top left), 29, 102 (middle)

SUSIE CUSHNER
page 75

REED DAVIS
pages 13, 45

RICHARD FELBER
page 61 (top left)

ROB FIOCCA
page 119

DANA GALLAGHER
pages 11 (left), 25 (left), 28, 54, 57 (right), 115,
117 (top row)

GENTL & HYERS
pages 7 (top center), 32 (top), 63, 69, 74, 82,
83, 91, 102 (top), 107, 124 (bottom right),
125 (top middle)

JOHN GRUEN
pages 12, 59, 62 (bottom), 84 (top), 92 (bottom),
118 (top row), 124 (top row)

LISA HUBBARD
pages 16 (bottom), 18, 25 (right), 35 (right two),
52, 53, 60, 96, 127 (middle)

THIBAULT JEANSON
pages 46-49, 93 (top row)

RICHARD GERHARD JUNG
pages 111 (top row), 117 (bottom)

MAX KIM BEE
page 35 (left two)

STEPHEN LEWIS
pages 81 (top), 92 (top and middle), 106 (top
and bottom left)

CHARLES MARAIA
pages 39, 123 (top)

WILLIAM MEPPEM
pages 34, 61 (bottom right)

JAMES MERRELL
pages 90, 129 (top row)

AMY NEUNSINGER
pages 11 (right), 38 (left), 55

VICTORIA PEARSON
pages 7 (top right, center, bottom left), 67,
73, 104 (right)

MARIA ROBLEDO
page 7 (bottom center and right)

DAVID PRINCE
pages 22 (top), 27 (left), 127 (bottom)

DAVID SAWYER
pages 93 (bottom), 111 (bottom), 125 (top left
and right, bottom), 126

CHARLES SCHILLER
pages 17, 66, 114

VICTOR SCHRAGER
pages 3, 26 (bottom), 88, 98, 99, 118 (bottom),
123 (bottom)

JOSE VAN RIELE
page 72 (bottom)

SIMON WATSON
pages 10 (right), 14, 36, 37, 79, 80

JONELLE WEAVER
page 78 (bottom row)

WENDELL T. WEBBER
pages 15, 16 (top row), 62 (top row), 86 (top
row), 127 (top)

ANNA WILLIAMS
pages 26 (top), 32 (all but top left), 33, 56 (right),
58, 64, 65, 72 (top), 81 (bottom row), 84 (bottom),
85, 86 (bottom), 87, 116

JAMES WORRELL
pages 1, 105, 130, 140, 142, 144

Front Cover:
SANG AN (top center)
CHRISTOPHER BAKER (all but top center)

Back Cover:
SANG AN (center left)
CHRISTOPHER BAKER (all but top right, cen-
ter left and center middle)
RICHARD GERHARD JUNG (center middle)
VICTOR SCHRAGER (top right)

"I have several large signal flags from a dealer who special-izes in vintage nautical salvage. I use them as tablecloths at summer parties—the bold, crisp colors and patterns look magnificent." *Kerri Mertaugh, Associate Home Editor* ✕ "Always have plenty of ice handy (we keep extra bags in the freezer)." *Jonathan Chernes, Creative Services Director* ✕ "Don't overlook the garage as a spillover space for parties. Park your car on the street, lay some temporary carpeting, be creative with the lighting, arrange tables and chairs, and you're all set—even when outdoor entertaining is challenged by a surprise rainstorm." *Steve Traut, Marketing Director* ✕ "Add flavor and a splash of color to drinks served in punch bowls or clear pitchers: Freeze berries or pieces of fruit submerged in water in small dessert bowls. Just before everyone arrives, unmold the ice from the bowl and add it to your punch." *Emily Anthon, Executive Assistant* ✕ "For a dinner party, let guests know it's BYOM—bring your own music. Put their CDs in your mixer and select random play. Everyone present will have familiar music they love, but will also be introduced to some they otherwise might not have heard."